Parables
for
Plain People
Observations of FooFoo the Wise

by

Jack Worrill

Copyright © 2010 by Jack Worrill

Parables for Plain People
Observations of FooFoo the Wise
by Jack Worrill

Printed in the United States of America

ISBN 9781609575212

All rights reserved solely by the author. The author guarantees all contents are original and do not infringe upon the legal rights of any other person or work. No part of this book may be reproduced in any form without the permission of the author. The views expressed in this book are not necessarily those of the publisher.

Unless otherwise indicated, Bible quotations are taken from The King James Bible; The Living Bible. Copyright © 1971 by Tyndale House Publishers (LB), Wheaton, Illinois 60187; and The Holy Bible, New International Version (NIV). Copyright © 1978 by New York International Bible Society.

www.xulonpress.com

Dedication

These Parables for Plain People…and all those to follow… are dedicated to my dear wife Lyn, who graduated into the Kingdom on January 26, 2010. They are dedicated as well to our three beautiful and dutiful daughters and their stalwart husbands, who are a great source of pride and joy, and have filled my quiver to overflowing with wonderful grandchildren and great-grandchildren. I wish the Lord's grace, peace and joy to each and all of you. And I claim the Lord's promise to be with you and provide for you in this life and into the next. (Psalm 37:25)

But First …

Before you read any further, I want to explain the title…and then the sub-title.

Many of the people who have read some or all of these Parables have asked why I insist on referring to them as "parables." I know… I was raised in Sunday School on the stories from the Bible and the parables of Jesus, and I often heard a parable defined as "an earthly story with a heavenly meaning." I have never had any illusion that my little—some have categorized them as meditations or devotions…I prefer to think of them as observations—my little observations should be compared to the Lord's marvelous insights.

At the same time, however the dictionary defines a parable as "A simple story illustrating a moral or religious lesson." The Greek roots literally mean "to throw beside." These writings usually begin with something I have observed or experienced, then, following some expansion of the original ideas, are wrapped up in a few lines of more or less spiritual application that are "thrown alongside." So, there you are. They are parables…at least to my mind.

Secondly, my dear mother-in-law, a retired English teacher, was one of the first to take exception to the designation "Plain People." She was concerned that would be a turn-off for some potential readers disinclined to think of themselves as "plain," in the sense of ordinary.

Well, I long ago gave up the delusion that I am anything other than plain. I once thought of myself as "smarter than the average bear." In my more mellow years, however, I have come to understand that the average bear is a lot smarter than he used to be. I'm just an ordinary, plain guy that the Lord occasionally zaps with an extra inspiration that is possibly worth sharing…and other plain people are the only ones likely to listen.

Next, our first Granddaughter was the one who nailed me with the nickname "FooFoo," because she couldn't imitate the "Yoo Hoo" whistle I used to call her with when she visited our house. When you can't whistle, you "foofoo," and I've been FooFoo to the grandkids ever since.

Finally, one day I was explaining something or other to another of the grandchildren, and when I finished he asked, "FooFoo, how did you get to be so wise?" Several times since then he has called me FooFoo the Wise. Not a bad image for a Grandfather to try to live up to, is it?

So there you have it. I'm sticking with "Parables for Plain People—Observations of FooFoo the Wise."

"Hear this, all ye peoples; give ear, all ye inhabitants of the
world, both low and high, rich and poor, together,
My mouth shall speak of wisdom,
and the meditation of my heart shall be of understanding.
I will incline mine ear to a parable..."
Psalm 49:1-4a

Parable of The Brick

It happens all the time, so I wasn't surprised when it happened again the other day. I needed something to put under the leg of the metal table outside the basement door. Something to even it up and keep it off the ground. As I looked through my "collection of stuff," I found just the thing: half a brick that I had salvaged for just such an occasion as this.

Around any recently-built house, if you poke around in the dirt you can find any number of bricks…whole or broken. When I come across them, I dig them out and stack them someplace handy. Of course, not everyone is a scavenger and a pack-rat like me. Most folks want to clean up and clear out what they think of as junk…to pick up and straighten up and get rid of all those odds and ends of stuff. Not me.

I can always find a use for an occasional brick; even half-bricks and larger scraps. I used to wonder why anyone would just throw away something as useful as a brick. (I have also thought it the height of wastefulness to throw perfectly good, used 2 x 4's and scraps of plywood…even five- or six-foot pieces of electrical cable, half a dozen shingles, the tail-end of a roll of roofing material…you know what I mean.) Nothing is as useful as a couple of bricks, or some 2 x 4 scraps or three feet of roofing felt, especially when that's all you need.

Certainly, it's true that when you're engaged in a real building, repair or remodeling project, a wheelbarrow full of bricks or a few beat-up boards are a waste of time. You can spend more time rehabilitating those scraps than they're worth. Not only that, but a few bricks just aren't good for much when you have ambitious plans.

Think about it. How much can you build with a couple of odd bricks? It's more economical to have new materials delivered on skids...then just throw away whatever is left over when you're finished with the project. At least that's true these days when time and labor are valued higher than materials. No wonder the contractors used to just dump those left-over bricks and wood scraps into a hole and cover them up (of course, most building codes won't allow them to do that today.)

In spiritual terms, however, the divine Builder values each brick, shingle and 2 x 4. True, a single brick may not seem so important by itself, but the Builder never makes His plans without taking the individual bricks—and their place in the total structure—into account.

The apostle Paul says we should think of ourselves as living stones, or bricks, each with a specific place in the Building planned by God. Each one, in its appointed place, makes the structure strong and beautiful.

When we are tempted to think of ourselves as insignificant and unimportant, we should recall that the failure or absence of a single brick is all it takes to bring down a might arch, to topple an imposing wall. Never think that your contribution doesn't matter...that your accomplishments don't count...where the work of the Lord is concerned.

The servant who buried his "bricks" in the back yard, instead of building something useful with them was called "wicked" when his master returned. "I didn't give you enough bricks to build a bridge or a building, but at least you could have built a nice barbecue pit." Or propped up a table.

Have you done anything useful with the bricks the Builder gave you? And, as one of His bricks, are you helping hold up your share of the load and presenting an attractive appearance to the world's "sidewalk superintendents"? Mind you, I'm not accusing...just asking.

Parable of The Cows and the Kids

Mr. Ray Smathers was the Minister of Music at Atlanta's First Baptist Church for many years. He once told of an early incident with his pre-school children's choir. They had just finished the last rehearsal before they were to sing in an important church program. When he had lined them up, he told them, "Now, remember who is on each side of you. When we go into the service tonight you are to stand next to the same people you're standing beside right now. I won't have time to rearrange you, so don't forget." Ray said one of the mothers was upset because he was expecting too much from children so young, and that it was unreasonable to make them responsible for lining themselves up.

Ray responded by relating an experience he had on his first holiday away from home with a college classmate, whose parents operated a dairy farm. He said that at milking time his friend took him out to the milking barn as the cows came in from the pasture. Each cow would amble into the building and down the wide center aisle, many of them passing up several un-occupied stalls before turning in to one.

Ray remarked that it seemed strange to him that they would not just turn in to the first vacant stall…if they chose to turn in at all. After all, he reasoned, they were just cows. He said his friend told him, "Oh, no, you don't understand. There is a stall assigned to each cow, and she is always milked in the same stall. Each one knows which stall is hers, and won't willingly stop in another cow's stall."

After a meaningful pause, Ray turned to the mother and said, "I think your child has as much sense as a cow...don't you?"

Motivational experts tell us that most people, especially children and teenagers, will behave exactly the way you expect them to. Generally speaking, if you treat them as if you expect them to be polite and orderly, they will respond. Treat them as if you expect them to be rude and unruly, and they will always oblige you.

It doesn't take a particularly astute observer to recognize that much of our society today is suffering from low expectations. Whether the subject is appropriate language, common courtesy, proper dress for special occasions, consideration for others...it seems that we have surrendered high ideals for the least common denominator, in order to accommodate those who are ignorant, lazy or self-indulgent. And it's our own fault.

The teachers I remember most clearly and with the greatest fondness—both in my school experience and since—are those who expected...indeed, would not accept less than...my best, whether in terms of dress, personal conduct or performance of the required tasks. The leaders we most respect are those who have established clear and reasonable standards—as well as clear and reasonable penalties for our failure to live up to them.

On the days when I am least satisfied with my performance, or that of others around me, I often realize that the reason is that I didn't make sure what was expected of me, or that I failed to explain what I was expecting.

Someone once said, "It is better to be sometimes cheated than to fail to trust." What we expect of others—what we trust them to do—should represent our high ideals for them. It's much better to insist on those ideals, even if they sometimes fall short.

I often wonder if I have made it clear to those around me what I expect of them; and, whether I have expected their best, or have settled for what they are willing to do with the least personal investment. I think I'll try to expect great things and take my chances with failure.

Parable of The Ego Pruners

Among the most important lessons we can learn in life is that we should never take ourselves too seriously. From the first time we're called upon to do "that cute little thing" we do for family, friends and new acquaintances—and especially for the parents of another child prodigy who has just done *his* cute little performance—we run the risk of being told how smart, talented and attractive we are. The trick is to hear all this praise without allowing it to deceive us into really believing it. In spite of our best efforts, we often need some assistance with the chore of keeping our egos pruned back to a healthy point. And whether for better or worse, there always seems to be a willing cadre of volunteers to take up the loppers and whack away.

A pair of personal experiences come to mind.

Every group has one. You recognize the type immediately. The self-appointed matriarch who has taken on the heavy burden of responsibility of being the primary arbiter of truth and wisdom, fashion and decorum for the group, and is not reluctant to hand down her judgments without respect to personalities.

We had one in our church choir in Greenwood, South Carolina. For those who are old enough to remember Al Capp's cartoon "Li'l Abner," she was a little like a female version of General Bullmoose, whose slogan was, "If it's good for Bullmoose, it's good for the world!" Her blessing was a coveted stamp of approval for many, and those she shunned…well, they just had to get along as best they could.

For some reason, she took a liking to me, and that's why I happened to be beside her on that Sunday when a soprano soloist from Lander College had the Special Music in the morning service. As the choir filed out of the choir loft following the service, our Mother Superior (I've always thought of her as Lady Bullmoose) turned to the young singer and pronounced sweetly, "That was such a pretty song!"

The young woman graciously thanked her and went on into the choir room. When she was out of earshot, Lady Bullmoose turned to me and said smugly, "I can always say it was a pretty song, even if I didn't particularly like the way it was sung."

A few weeks later I had the privilege of singing the Special Music in the morning service, and was reasonably pleased with my presentation. That is, I was until I was approached by Lady Bullmoose, who told me grandly, "That was *such* a pretty song!" Since then I have made a point of not being too heavily invested in the praise and approval of the general audience. Once you understand the code, it's not too difficult to keep your ego the proper size.

That reminds me of the time I experienced the fastest inflation and deflation of ego that one could ever imagine. We were in that same church in South Carolina, and our first little girl was only a few months old. She was beautiful, of course, with a lovely smile, and blue eyes just like mine. When one of our friends remarked,

"Well, I can see she got her looks from her daddy…" I began to levitate. I was quickly returned to earth, however, when she finished, "…because her mother still has hers." The Lord has many ways to keep us humble, if we only pay attention.

Parable of One Who Would Lead

There is a story that comes from the days of the Westward expansion by early settlers, about a long line of covered wagons making its way across the Great American Prairie. For many days and weeks they followed the faintly visible track of the wagon trains that had gone before them, through the waving grasses, around rock formations and boggy lowlands, crossing creeks, streams and the occasional river.

Every morning, as the Number One wagon would strike out along the trail, the wagon master's dog would take his position twenty or thirty paces ahead and proudly "lead the way," from time to time sniffing the dusty tracks and looking back over his shoulder as if to say, "It's all right folks...we're on the right trail." That had been his routine ever since the caravan had set out from St. Louis, Missouri.

Then came the day when the hopeful travelers reached a fork in the trail, one branch turning north toward the Colorado territory and the other bearing more southerly, bound for California. The dog, after pausing briefly and dutifully sniffing first the northern track and then the southern one, chose the Colorado leg and confidently resumed his stride-sniff-and-look routine. He hadn't gotten very fat—perhaps fifty or sixty yards up the trail—before he sniffed and turned to check out his charges...only to discover that the wagons had taken the other leg, heading to California.

Faced with this blatant challenge to his leadership, he barked sharply three times, turned and walked about fifteen steps up *his* trail, then turned to see if his humans had corrected their error and followed his lead. When it became evident they were not going to leave the trail they had chosen, he sat briefly, as if contemplating the frailty of the human brain, then resignedly and with great dignity cut across the expanse of waving grass to once more resume his position as faithful trailblazer and guide, which he maintained all the way to California.

It is true—as it has always been—not all who stand out front are leaders. Being a leader is so much more than being the one at the head of the line. It is not Leadership to tentatively precede the crowd as they go where they want.

I have heard it said that this is one of the principal distinctions between a Politician and a Statesman. The first "leads" wherever his constituents want to go. The second leads in the direction dictated by his convictions, many times dragging his constituents, kicking and screaming, behind him. The typical Politician is more often re-elected than the Statesman.

The true Leader sets his eye on the goal, convinced of the proper path to achieve it, and then sets the pace, following that path with conviction…even if he must begin alone.

Parable of One Who Would Lead—Part 2

Cody first appeared in our neighborhood as a scrawny, quivering stray. Some of the kids told me that he was teased and tormented a good bit, so he was understandably wary of the approach of any human…so it was only because he was on the verge of starving that we were able to get near him, and then only if we offered food.

His first connection with our family was when everyone had gathered to help me forget my fiftieth birthday. Cody must have smelled the food and been unable to resist his hunger in spite of all the people. Even in his emaciated condition he was a beautiful animal. We later guessed that he was mostly English Setter, white with tan patches.

Our daughter had just started working for a nearby veterinary clinic and took him on as a sort of project. She took him to obedience classes at the clinic, but, being a typical teen, seldom had the time…or inclination…to practice with him, so he only learned what he wanted to learn.

I'll always remember seeing her taking him down the driveway for his walks. At the command "Heel!" Cody would charge down the drive at the extreme end of his lead, like the lead sled dog heading for Iditarod. With every other step she would shout "Heeeel!" and Cody would continue to tow with all his strength. Thus entered into the family lexicon the expression "The Cody Heel and Tow."

When our daughter moved into an apartment of her own, Cody was well past the emaciated and undernourished state he was in when he took us as his pets. However, that also meant that he was over the maximum size for pets allowed by her rental contract. Since then Cody has been ours—or vice versa—and I've been the one to take him for his tugs each day.

In the early days we would strike out for his—and my—workout, with the lead so taut it almost whistled in the breeze…the choke chain so tight that Cody's breathing sounded like the laboring of a steam engine…and with me, striving to maintain the dignified appearance of a leisurely stroll with man's best friend, occasionally lunging here or there as the lead dog decided to change direction.

I could tell when it was time to turn back when I could keep up with him without that half-running-half-walking gait that his brand of leadership dictated. By the time we arrived back at the house he paced along with the bearing of General Patton entering Paris in the lead tank, as if he had just liberated the neighborhood.

Cody was only a couple of years old then. Now he is over fifteen. I understand that is quite elderly for his breed. He is nearly deaf and blind, and arthritis has afflicted his hind quarters so that he has trouble betting onto all fours. These days I nearly have to shout to let him know it's time to go out for our walk. I have to fetch the lead off the shelf myself, because it's just out of his reach since he can't get up on his hind legs, and his rear end doesn't always support him long enough for him to get it.

Our walks are much shorter now. Cody still strikes out with all the vigor he can muster, but now his leadership style has changed considerably. He spends most of the walking time sniffing all the landmarks—I call it checking his "P"-mail—and leaving little memos of his own. The lead is so slack I constantly have to watch to be sure he doesn't trip over it.

When he has seen, sniffed and done all he needs, he will turn behind me and head back up the street to his house in a slow, deliberate "mosey." No more saving the neighborhood...no heroics...just doing what is necessary to get it over with.

Cody has adopted a new philosophy of leadership. He doesn't fight the lead now. In fairness, he doesn't "Heel!" either, but if it weren't for the County's leash laws we could go for our walks without bothering with the lead. He is quite willing to let others bear the burden of keeping the neighborhood safe for civilization while he just does what is necessary. He walks as if he were reminiscing about the good old days when he kept things in order.

Life has a lot of lessons for those who would lead. Many of us start out straining at the leash, expecting to accomplish great things that will influence masses of people. We rush onward with great expenditure of energy and enthusiasm, trying to fix everything, help everyone, solve all problems. It's not easy saving the world—it's tiring, it's perplexing, it's frustrating...and, we must finally admit, it's impossible.

If we really would lead, though, we need to learn that the important accomplishments, for all but an elite few, are to be realized within the small, intimate sphere of influence where we spend our daily lives. As we mature we realize that the masses we dreamed of impressing aren't very important in the final scheme of things. Most of us will influence the lives of far more people than we imagine, but seldom are they the ones we thought we would come to care about.

We could all take a tip from Cody. Relax, don't take our selves or others too seriously. In the words of one motivational speaker I heard recently, "Take it easy. Do what you can. Can what you do…and sit on your can!"

And, by the way, don't feel too sorry for Cody with all his ailments and the frailties of his advancing age. He knows someone is providing for his needs. He spends his days around the people he knows care for him. His human pets are pretty well housebroken, and fairly forgiving when he forgets to be. And he's still got all his teeth. Whether dog or human, how much better does it get than that?

Parable of Pals and Puppies

Mac and I have known each other since ninth grade and been best friends since ur Junior year at North Fulton High School. In our Senior year we were room-mates on the Special Choir tour to New Orleans. One night, after we were supposed to be asleep, we were talking softly across the room to each other about those deep philosophical questions that occupy the minds of all adolescents: the meaning of life; how to achieve world peace, how to benefit mankind, whether that cute girl knows we exist, could acne actually prove fatal…all the important stuff.

We eventually got around to discussing our feelings of inadequacy. And, since we were authorities on each other's inadequacies, we felt free to give honest, unvarnished opinions of how we could improve ourselves.

I distinctly remember discussing a solo I had sung recently— Besame Mucho, in Spanish. Mac's sensitive advice to me, as I recall, was something to the point that I shouldn't give up my day job…if and when I ever got one.

I also remember Mac asking why a particular clique at school didn't seem to welcome him. My learned pronouncement from atop Mount Jack was that perhaps it was because, in his eagerness to make a good impression, he was a bit like a Saint Bernard puppy that bounds up with muddy feet and jumps up on an unprepared visitor. I suggested that he back off a bit and not act as if that clique's acceptance was so important to him. I think I must have read that somewhere. I don't know if the advice was any good, but Mac turned out all right, anyway.

Years later, having successfully survived adolescence, Mac acquired a Saint Bernard puppy and named it McDonald. I never thought to ask Mac if that was merely a coincidence. Anyway, as if to prove ancient prophecy, McDonald did tend to intimidate visitors, although his master no longer did so.

When I think of enthusiastic creatures, I also think of my grand-puppy, Sonny. He belongs to our daughter MaKay and her family. Part dachshund, part unidentifiable hound, Sonny always welcomes guests with yelps of delight and an excited happy dance. And, at least whenever I am the visitor, his enthusiasm usually runneth over, wetting my pants-leg and shoe as well as the floor and the occasional piece of furniture.

Now don't get me wrong. I can appreciate an enthusiastic greeting as much as the next guy. But there are limits, social rules about these things. I guess my point is that almost anything can be overdone. Even good things.

I was once asked why I didn't enjoy a certain music program, since I like that particular type of music. I answered, "Well, I like canned peaches, too, but I don't sit down and eat an institutional-size can at one sitting." The Bible tells us that everything God created is good, but meant to be enjoyed in moderation. Actually, I believe the only things not meant to be applied moderately are what we call the Spiritual Gifts: love, joy, peace, patience, kindness, goodness, faithfulness, gentleness and self-control. There are no rules to limit these...nor should there be.

Parable of The Pastor's Box

My pastor is a striking young man, and an excellent preacher. His tall, slender appearance in the pulpit is very commanding. His deep, clear, booming voice is reminiscent of the charismatic pulpiteers of old who have shaped our church history. However, when he sits on the steps of the pulpit platform with the children of the congregation, his voice is soft and gentle like the loving father he is; his thoughts simple and clearly expressed.

For his children's messages, he has begun a practice which challenges his creativity and tests his ability to communicate a meaningful inspirational thought to the eager children who crowd around him. Each Sunday he bestows the Pastor's Box on one of the children to be brought back the next week with something that has special meaning to the young recipient. The only limitation is that it can't be alive...or even recently alive. Then, he takes the object each week and extemporaneously crafts an object lesson around it. His thoughts have been insightful and well received by both young and old listeners.

When he sat with the children on the Sunday after Valentine's Day and asked for the Pastor's Box, its contents weren't a complete surprise. He reached in and retrieved a typical "school box" valentine. His message, built around that simple little card with its usual sentimental words, focused on the importance of our love and care for each other. He did his usual good job and the children went their way with another spiritual gem to guide them.

As usual, though, I began to think of how I would have handled that opportunity. What would I have made of the Valentine from the Pastor's Box? My approach would have been a little different, I think.

My first impression upon seeing that valentine was not of my love for that "special someone," but, rather, of the love of Jesus for us all. The traditional heart shape reminded me of His heart, filled to breaking with that love. And of His love so overwhelming that it could touch us all, and make change possible. His love is so great that the only way one man can begin to imitate it is to be willing to die for the one who is the object of that love.

My next thought was of the importance of a healthy, beating heart in the continuation of life. The heart is so important that in some cases the only hope is to have a diseased one removed and a healthy one transplanted in its place. Once a medical miracle, the heart transplant has become almost commonplace, extending life for many.

However, much more important than the physical heart transplant—as crucial as that may be—is the spiritual heart transplant which faith in Jesus affords. Through His love for us, which led Him to surrender His life in payment for the penalty of our sin, He has offered us a new heart with the enriched life it brings to all who accept it.

Honestly, if I had been the one pulling that valentine from the Pastor's Box, I probably wouldn't have thought quickly enough to clearly express my thoughts about Jesus' loving heart, and the transplant He offers. But maybe I'll get the chance to tell someone today.

Parable of Patchwork

It was just one of a multitude of boxes we went through when we emptied Grandmother's house. Sorting through all those boxes of unused things had been a chore and this one was only a brief curiosity a the time.

I remembered that box recently as an antique patchwork quilt caught my eye. The quilt was definitely not a "crazy quilt," made up of countless unmatched cloth remnants randomly stitched together with no obvious pattern or color scheme in mind. This quilt was beautifully designed, the colored bits of cloth were perfectly matched, sewn with tiny stitches that clearly indicated a sharp eye and steady hand, as well as a patience and persistence that are not found in abundance today.

Our family has enjoyed the use of many such quilts—a dozen or more in all sizes and in a wide range of patterns. All of them, obviously handmade and already well worn with years of use, salvaged from the treasure trove of Grandmother's house. People tell us what a valuable collection we have in that lot of antique quilts. We couldn't ever sell them, though. Use them, enjoy them, show them to friends, wear them our, perhaps…but sell them? Not likely.

That was plainly the type of quilt Grandmother intended to make when she started setting aside the fragments we found in that box. It contained hundreds of pieces and scraps of cloth—little triangles, squares and rectangles, carefully color-matched and grouped by shape and size—material for a patchwork pattern long forgotten.

Some of the pieces of fabric were new, scraps that fell to the floor when some scissors-wielding seamstress cut away whatever didn't look like the dress, shirt or other creation she had n mind. Other cloth was plainly salvaged from garments or curtains or other things that had outlived their original usefulness. And Grandmother, never one to throw anything away except under severe duress, determined to put all these little segments to use—"waste not" as they said, and believed, in her generation. The wise ones among us would do well to follow that example.

It made me smile to remember that box of patchwork elements. Someone had taken a lot of time putting together the darks and lights called for in the pattern. The colors and patterns needn't match exactly. Green is green, blue is blue, plaid is plaid, print is print, and "close enough is good enough." But when everything has been assembled there is an obvious unity about the selections that makes the pattern clearly evident.

It also makes me smile to realize that my life is a lot like one of those artistically conceived and crafted quilts. I am certain that the Creator collected all the bits and pieces needed to make me into the form that suited His plan. Not a crazy quilt randomly tacked together willy-nilly…without rhyme or reason—no matter what the evolutionists among us might declare. No, but just like Grandmother's masterpieces, carefully and purposefully assembled, with each element selected for its maximum contribution to the final product, faithful to the Maker's perfect pattern.

Some of those scraps and fragments are old and familiar... coming from family personality traits—or traditions whose origins are lost in the cloudy past. Today's science tells us that most of what we are is already programmed into our genes, carefully tucked away in our DNA. Some of the material that makes my personality unique comes from "new cloth"—experiences selected by the Lord to bring a certain special quality that will complete the perfect pattern He has planned for me.

The important lesson in the Parable of Patchwork is that the elements that make up and shape our lives are not the result of chance. The Lord uses all the events of life—the good and the bad—as raw materials to craft something beautiful in us that will bring Him pleasure.

Finally, just as surely as each of those quilts has a beauty that is pleasing to the eye, they were also designed and crafted with a functional purpose...to keep the people warm. No matter how attractive they were, they wouldn't have been kept around for long if they didn't do the job for which they were intended. To paraphrase the Apostle Paul, "For we are His patchwork, created in Christ Jesus to good works...that we should walk in them." (Ephesians 2:10)

So why not go out today, attract someone with your pleasant design, then wrap yourself around them and warm their heart? I dare you.

Parable of **The Poem**

When I was in about the fifth grade, I read a poem that really inspired me. It was in one of those American Literature books that collected excerpts and short works of all sorts; poetry and prose illustrating examples of the many ways writers express themselves.

I can't explain why I found this particular poem so appealing, but I decided that I wanted to preserve it in a special way. Since carving it in stone was out of the question…I didn't have a big enough stone, didn't know how to carve and, at that age, didn't have the time, skill or patience…I reached the only logical conclusion: ask Dad to fix it for me.

My Dad was in the printing business—more accurately, the Direct Mail Advertising business—and could do anything. He had artists and typesetters and printing presses all at his disposal, and he knew how to do everything. I was certain of that, at age eleven.

So, one evening I went over to his chair during his daily ritual of reading and absorbing every word of the Atlanta Journal, and made my request. As I recall, I was eloquent in my description of the poem and its significance to me. I was also careful to explain why he was so imminently qualified to help me preserve this important work of literature. What I wanted wasn't really so difficult for someone with his resources to provide, was it?

All I wanted was one copy…with one of those ornate, flowery borders, and elegant, decorative initial letters at the beginning of each verse…you know, like the illuminated manuscripts you see in old books and things like that. That would really be a cool way to immortalize such a literary gem, don't you think?

What I didn't know, or care about at age eleven, was that to fulfill my request would have been outrageously expensive. An artist would have to devote many hours to the illustration. Type, before the age of computer-generated fonts, would have to be set by hand. Color separations, multiple passes through the printing press, expensive vellum paper—and all for one copy. But I had no idea or concern about how many hundreds of dollars it would have cost. I only knew I wanted my poem.

I don't know whether his solution was out of his fatherly wisdom, or merely instinctive self-defense, but it made an impression that has lasted to this day. He told me that, of course, he had all the people, materials and equipment to print the type of manuscript I wanted, but he had a better idea.

Dad's counsel was this: "If you really want to preserve something in a way that you can keep forever, that you can never lose, and that will never deteriorate or be taken from you, the thing to do is to memorize it. I could never print anything that would be as beautiful or as permanent as what you can keep in your imagination. Memorize it, son, that's the best way."

So I did. And, among all the words or wisdom and all the excellent, sound advice Dad gave me, that has proven to be some of the best. The poem, "The Way to Win," still holds an honored place in the halls of my memory, having lost none of its luster, unstained by years of use. No matter that I have never again seen it in print; nor can I give credit to the author, whose name I didn't learn. But I do bring it out and "read" it often. And it still inspires me.

The Way to Win

It takes a little courage, and a little self-control,
And some grim determination, if you want to reach the goal.
It takes a deal of striving with a stern and firm-set chin,
No matter what the battle, if you're really out to win.

There's no easy path to glory, there's no rosy road to fame.
Life, however you may view it, is no simple parlor game.
But its prizes call for fighting, for endurance and for grit;
For a rugged disposition, and a don't-know-when-to-quit.

You must take a blow or give one. You must win and you must lose,
And expect that in the battle you will suffer from a bruise.
But you mustn't wince or falter, if the fight you once begin.
Be a man and face the battle. That's the only way to win!

- Author Unknown

Parable of **The Shared Blessing**

My Dad spent a large part of his Christian life in Southern Baptist churches doing Lay preaching, teaching Lay Evangelism Schools and leading Lay-led Revivals in churches of all sizes. He got started doing these things while he was active in the Baptist Brotherhood, the men's missionary organization in the Baptist Church, and because he had developed an interest in personal evangelism.

Whenever Dad was to lead a week-long Lay Evangelism School, it was his practice to preach a sermon on the preceding Sunday, to lay the spiritual ground-work for it and generate as much enthusiasm among the members of the congregation as possible. On one occasion, after preaching the "pep talk" sermon in a small rural church in South Georgia, Dad was standing at the front door with the pastor, shaking the hands of the members as they departed. There was the typical repertoire of responses, the "amen's," the promises to attend, as well as the legitimate reasons…and the occasional lame excuse… for not being able to be present.

Among those who came up to shake his hand was an elderly woman, very plainly dressed and soft-spoken, who praised his message and his ministry and thanked him for his willingness to help her and her church friends do a better job in personal witnessing. When she took her hand away from his, she left a tightly-rolled dollar bill in his palm.

To understand what happened next, it is important to know that Dad had been quite successful in his Direct Mail business. He was well respected in the community, he had a nice, though not ostentatious, home, matching Cadillacs for himself and his wife; he always paid all his own expenses whenever he went on his Lay preaching and teaching trips.

That's why, when he realized that this sweet woman, a widow on Social Security and with very meager means, had pressed a dollar bill into his hand he was embarrassed. That dollar, which wasn't enough for a respectable tip in the places where he usually ate, was quite a lot for someone in her financial condition. He gently insisted that she take it back, as a gift from him, and do something with it for herself.

The pastor, who had served that church for many years, looked on without saying anything. However, as soon as they were alone in his study, he softly but firmly rebuked my father for what he had just done. He said, "Fred, what you did out there was a selfish and thoughtless thing. That dollar bill may not mean much to you, but it was wrong for you to refuse to accept it from her. Do you realize that you were denying her a blessing—the blessing of giving something she valued, as an expression of her gratitude for what you are doing? I hope you don't ever do that again, Brother."

That was an important lesson for Dad, which he passed on to me. It is good to be reminded once in a while that there is a proper time to be the "bless-er" and also a time to allow oneself to be the "bless-ee." Truly enough, Jesus did say it is more blessed to give than to receive; but in order for someone to give, someone must also be prepared to receive...to share the blessing. May God give us the grace to recognize the difference.

When someone wants to do something nice for you, put ego aside. Be gracious and prepare to share the blessing. I've discovered that every time I have been willing to share the blessing it has just grown in value, leaving me doubly blessed.

Parable of The Drownproofer

He had a voice that could etch glass. It was a voice that could easily be heard by someone at the bottom of the deep end of the swimming pool. And, I suppose, that was the point. I remember clearly hearing that voice on one occasion, while drifting halfway between the bottom and the surface of the pool…with my hands and feet tied. Even under water, it was as piercing as the cry of a red-tailed hawk announcing its presence. He shrieked, "Blow, sucker!"

One couldn't hear that voice and not respond, so I obediently blew out all my air, sank dutifully to the pool bottom and pushed off as I had been taught. That propelled me to the surface for a gasp of air, and I continued to swim the required distance to pass the "Fifteen Yards with Hands and Feet Tied" skill. I'll always remember, and be grateful for, the winter quarter of my Freshman year and the Physical Training Survival Swimming course. We called it Drownproofing 102.

The instructor was Fred Lanoue, who had coached the Georgia Tech swimming team for many years. However, his main claim to fame is that he developed a water survival technique that has saved countless lives since it was first taught to sailors in the U. S. Navy during World War II. As a young swimming instructor, he was horrified to learn of all the sailors who drowned in the South Pacific during the early months of the war. It seems that most of the deaths occurred simply because the victims had not been taught one basic scientific fact.

That fact is that roughly 97% of the world's population have a body density less than that of water. In other words, almost everybody is naturally buoyant. Without any effort we will naturally float. (In fact, some individuals are so buoyant that some of the underwater swimming skills taught in the drownproofing course could only be accomplished if they held a rubber brick in each hand to keep them on the bottom of the pool.)

The vast majority of drowning deaths occur from panic and fatigue, not because the victims cannot float. Traditional techniques have always called for treading water, which quickly drains energy; or floating on one's back, which can lead to swallowing large quantities of water, causing choking and hysteria.

One of the most liberating experiences of my life came when, while doing the so-called dead man's float in the center of the pool, I lowered my chin to touch my chest and felt the crown of my head go above the water's surface. All I had to do then was to raise my head, and my nose and mouth were out of the water, allowing me to take a breath. Before long, I was able to survive in the pool with my hands and feet tied for over an hour. After that I knew that if I was conscious I could survive in the water even without the use of my hands and feet. I was drownproof. Wow!

I have thought of that experience many times as I have dealt with problems in my life. When faced with difficulties, my natural tendency is probably the same as yours...to struggle and fight against the situation, trying to "stay afloat." I work as hard as I can, trying to remove the obstacles separating me from my goals, and they won't budge. I try to break through, burrow under, leap over or dash around. But, no matter how determined my efforts, there are always some obstacles that cannot be eliminated or overcome.

When I've come to the end of my resources...when my best efforts are ineffective...when my mind is muddled and I can't think of any solution...when I feel as if I'm sinking...that's when I finally pay attention to that voice within me that says, "Blow, sucker! Relax, and let My providence keep you afloat." And, you know what? After all these years, I'm beginning to trust the Lord's Law of Spiritual Buoyancy to keep me afloat. I'm better able to resist the panic that wastes my resources, efforts and mental energies. Even though I seem to be adrift and there's no help in sight, I can actually relax and rest.

Why not? I'm spiritually drownproof!

Parable of The Jar of Fleas

It has been a long time, now, since I first heard the story about the Jar of Fleas. I don't remember the name of the speaker at that Civitan Club meeting, or the other two of his "three points and a stirring conclusion" message. Except that I think one of them had to do with a bag of pump handles...or something like that. Anyway...

Here's the story as I remember it: There was once a researcher studying fleas. He collected a large number of them and kept them in a Mason jar. You know, the kind of jar folks use for canning, to preserve the season's fruits and vegetables to be enjoyed later.

He would punch a few air holes in the lid and observe them, taking notes as he watched. He did much of his research in the late evening and early morning, when the laboratory was quiet and there were few interruptions. Early one morning, as he worked on his notes, he heard a sound that he hadn't noticed before. It was an irregular, but definite "plink...plink, plink...plink..." coming from the jar of fleas.

After a period of patiently studying the jar, he discovered what he thought was the source of the noise. It appeared to be made by the fleas striking the metal lid of the jar as they jumped. Whenever he put a new batch of fleas into the jar, there would be an hour or so of these plinking sounds. However, after a while he noticed that the noise would gradually diminish, and eventually stop altogether.

As a scientist, he felt compelled to determine what could be learned from this interesting phenomenon. He monitored many batches of fleas, took copious notes; and this was his conclusion: Each new batch of fleas, not accustomed to being confined, would jump and hop as they always had, often jumping high enough to bat their little flea heads on the lid, resulting in the plinking sound he had first detected. He theorized that after a brief period of adjustment, however, the fleas learned how high they could jump and yet avoid the sudden headache caused by these collisions with the confining lid.

The scientist tested his theory by putting a new batch of fleas in the jar and waiting until the familiar noise ended. Then he slowly and carefully removed the lid, fully expecting to have the entire batch of fleas escape. As he studied the jar with a magnifying glass, however, he could see that, indeed, the fleas were visible jumping up to the level even with the top of the jar, but no higher. In other words, the fleas had learned how to accept their captivity and avoid its pain.

I don't know if this story is true or not—I suspect it's just a fanciful tale. but you have to admit that it has close parallels in our everyday lives. A great deal of life is spent in what we might characterize as "making the best of a bad situation," simply accepting unavoidable circumstances and trying to adapt them to our greatest advantage. We all spend a big part of our existence learning not to jump so high that we bump our little heads on the jar lid of Life.

But we're not fleas...and the Creator didn't intend for us to be confined in any of life's jars. And He certainly didn't intend for us to adapt ourselves so as to be more comfortable in those jars. In a commentary about the Prodigal Son, one author wrote, "God wanted to get the Prodigal *out* of the pig-pen, *not* to make him more comfortable there."

So, we have a choice. We can be like the fleas in the jar. We can make ourselves as content as possible in the confinement of the jar, and learn how to control our jumping activities so as to avoid the unpleasant "lid" experience. Or, we can be like the creatures the Maker fashioned, enjoying the freedom of life as He intended it, using the abilities He built into us to jump as high and as far as we can. I don't know about you, but I vote for life outside the jar.

Parable of **The Lasting Love**

What a great idea. And in such a perfect setting, too. A quaint little garden bench, with its own graffiti already supplied, alongside a winding stone path. The walkway continued through the open gate of a low, whitewashed garden fence, and behind the bench was an ancient, gnarled evergreen of some sort. A small stone fountain, a bird bath and a modest scattering of daffodils (or jonquils, I never can remember which is which) completed the scene.

This idyllic setting was just a small corner of the booth of a landscaper friend of ours, surrounded by a multitude of larger and more elaborate designs by exhibitors from all over the Southeast, at the Garden and Patio Show. But I just had to stop and absorb the quiet, insistent message that was inscribed on the back of the bench. Some vines and twigs fashioned into something like a heart-shaped pillow were on the seat, and beside a small hole, also heart-shaped, cut in the back of the bench, appeared the message that touched my heart: I Love You.

My first thought when I saw this striking little tableau hidden away in the bustle of the exhibition, was that it would make a perfect Valentine's Day message for my wife. I took photos from several angles, trying for one that would be the most effective. When I told the designer what I had in mind, she suggested that I let her take a picture of me sitting on the bench. So, when I began to sort through my photos, I had two sets of pictures—one set with just the bench and its enduring message…one with me seated beside the message, "I Love You."

I printed and framed the one with me on the "Love" bench and gave it to Lyn as my Valentine this year. No additional card…no message…just the photo. It said it all, I think.

Then as I looked at the two pictures, my mind began to wander off the path of romance and meander among other possible messages they suggested. I remembered the "Kilroy was here" graffiti irreverently inscribed in surprising places all around the world, supposedly by American GI's after World War II…evidence that they had in fact been there.

Whenever one comes across the signature of George P. Burdell on a membership roster, visitor's book or mailing list, there is the good chance it was put there as a joke. That was the pseudonym assumed by the perennial phantom freshman at Georgia Tech many decades ago. It is a clear sign that a Georgia Tech alumnus has been on the scene.

I remember seeing in the Boy Scout Handbook instructions for blazing a trail and leaving signs that others can recognize and identify, so they can follow the path you have explored. The markings say "I was here, and this is the way I went. Come, follow me."

I suppose that I didn't really have to give my wife the picture with me in it. All she needed to see was the words "I Love You," and she knew it was from me. Whether she can see me or not, she has the assurance of my lasting love…love that will last long after the inscription fades from that bench. Long after the bench itself is no more.

My mind is still meandering, and now I think, "That's just what God's love is like, isn't it?" One doesn't have to be particularly perceptive to recognize Godly graffiti all around us every day. His "I Love You" is evident to anyone who will just take a moment to look and listen...even in periods of pain, gloom or deepest despair...in the colors, smells and sounds of each day.

The song of a bird can brighten the dreariest day. The trusting hug of a child can restore fractured confidence and break depression's strangle-hold. There is no circumstance so dire that we can't hear that still, small Voice affirm, "Don't be afraid. I Love You." But we must listen.

For those who do, whether He is visible in the picture or not, the Lord's message is the same. "I have loved you with an everlasting love." (Jeremiah 31:3) Say "Amen!" somebody.

Parable of The Leaders of Cheer

It was mid-morning of a day about the end of March, when I went out to put something in the mailbox. It had begun as a gloomy, overcast day with a half-hearted chill in the air, only slightly reminiscent of the bitter cold that had characterized most of the Winter.

The driveway was strewn with pine straw and dry brown leaves long parted from the bare limbs and branches of the many trees in the yard. The grass was also brown, a shade only a little lighter than the leaves.

Just about the only color in the yard came from a profusion of wild violets scattered about the lawn, and especially along both edges of the driveway. They looked like two rows of picketers holding up green, heart-shaped signs to protest the unfairness of the cold weather, complaining about the delay of a long-promised Spring. As I passed between them I thought, "Right on, brothers!" and gave a mental "thumbs-up" of support and encouragement. "Come on, Spring!" I said softly, after looking around to be sure that no one was there to hear me.

Later that day, as if yielding to the pressure of plant opinion, perhaps in order to avoid violet demonstrations, the sun came out, the clouds dispersed and the afternoon was warm and beautiful. Everything appeared to be completely different when I again made the trip to the mailbox. True, the leaves and pine straw were still brown, the grass still looked pitiful, but the bright sunlight brought out texture and flecks of color that weren't noticeable before.

I also noticed that the violets along the driveway and dispersed around the lawn had really changed. Whereas in the gloom of the overcast morning the heart-shaped leaves of protest were all I noticed, now their appearance was completely different. Raised high above the leaves was a blanket of delicate blossoms, newly unfurled, a quiet riot of deep lavender, blue and white.

It was almost as if the plants in the yard were cheering, elated by the apparent success of their peaceful demonstration. They might as well have been applauding the Sun's work and waving their brightly colored banners of inspiration to all of us who had begun to wonder if Spring would ever come. In my mind they were like a band of tiny mimes, dressed in green, faces painted purple and white, doing their impression of cheerleaders shouting, "Let's hear it for Spring!" The thought made me chuckle and say, "Bless you, little leaders of cheer."

We all have those days when we need something to inspire us, give us a reason to hope that things will be better. When those days come, it is important for us to look around for these signs of promise. I've learned that the clues are all around us, if we diligently seek them out.

Recently, our then two-year-old granddaughter Emily spent the night with us. She asked for a toy, and, as we had done with her mother before her, I asked, "What do you say?" After a moment's thought she sweetly said, "Pleeeeeeeze." I gave her the toy, then asked, "Now what do you say?" A furrowed brow and tiny frown darkened her face for a second, then the eyes twinkled and a big grin lit her face as she shouted, "Hooray! You did it!" Not exactly the response I expected, but effective, just the same.

Every day it seems we are bombarded by reports of events which threaten our property, our health, our feeling of safety and security. It is easy to become discouraged, to lose that sense of joy and well-being that makes it possible to face the future with excitement and anticipation.

At just such times, the One who created us, and provides for us with His overwhelming love and sense of humor, finds a way to send us His word of hope. It may be through the sudden appearance of flowers, the exuberant singing of birds…perhaps even the unexpected "Hooray!" of a child…but He will send His leaders of cheer to those faithful ones who are waiting to hear.

Parable of The Smooth Stone

In our family, there is one common definition for both "vacation" and "beach." For each of them, the definition is "Pawleys Island." For ten consecutive years our family rented the same house at Pawleys with our friends the Willises. That week, and sometimes two, set the standard by which all of our family experiences have been measured since those years when our children were small. And I must observe that most family occasions A.P. (After Pawleys) have suffered from the comparison—perhaps not all, but certainly most.

Pawleys Island is small—only about a mile and a half long by a quarter of a mile or so wide. It was originally used by the rice planters of the Waccamaw Neck, in the South Carolina low country between Georgetown and Myrtle Beach, as a summer refuge for their families from the oppressive heat and threat of mosquito-borne fever. During the summers when we visited, there were a dozen or more houses that dated back to those plantation days. However, since Hurricane Hugo visited Pawleys several years ago, there are only a few of them left.

When we were regulars there, Pawleys wasn't the kind of place one visited expecting to see a lot of sights or engage in productive activities. On the other hand, we didn't return from there feeling as if we needed another vacation to recover before going back to work. The island had no shops or restaurants. The Pawleys Pavilion was the last place for entertainment, and it burned to the pilings in the '40's, I think.

There was no air conditioning in our house. No television or telephone, either. Our only communication medium was the radio we took so my wife Lyn, the group's official weather worrier, could keep track of thunderstorms, the occasional hurricane, and other night terrors.

That's the beauty of it. There was nothing to do...unless one wanted to swim in the surf, sun on the sand, walk on the beach (about an hour's purposeful walk to either end of the island and back), read a book, work a jigsaw puzzle, talk, nap or eat. Since we all joined in sharing the cooking, cleaning, shopping and babysitting chores, the work load was bearable. What a Paradise!

When we drove across the causeway and unloaded the car, I would take off my wrist watch, belt, and shoes and socks, and change into shorts. And none of those signs of responsible adulthood was donned again until we once more crossed the causeway, back into the civilized rat-race. On the mainland, we could eat fresh seafood, or shop for groceries at Lachicotte's Store. And for gifts and knick-knacks there was The Hammock Shop, home of the famous Pawleys Island Hammock. One could drive up to Myrtle Beach, but that defeated the purpose.

My usual morning ritual was to arise about 5:30 and go out to walk the beach. I've said many times since then that there is something therapeutic in looking back the way you have come and seeing no footprints but your own. On those walks I developed a knack for finding all sorts of treasures imported by the tide and deposited upon the newly scrubbed sand for the amusement and amazement of island visitors. Sand dollars, lady slippers, keyhole limpets, sea pens...beautiful and amazing discoveries were there in fresh abundance each morning.

One of the last mornings I walked there, before we had to stop going, I found something I have carried with me ever since. I spotted in the sand a smooth black stone with white criss-crosses imbedded in it. It had been tumbled in the sand for such a long time that it looked like one of those little rocks called a worry stone—almost. It wasn't flawless and brightly polished like those you can buy in the gem shops. It had a kind of satin finish, and a couple of ragged, bumpy places that were yet to be smoothed out. But it had the potential to be one of the prettiest and most unusual rocks I had ever seen...after just a little more grinding.

I've carried that imperfect stone, with all its potential for beauty, because it reminds me of myself. I have come to realize that I have within me a lot of potential that hasn't yet been brought out. Oh, I'm not nearly as ragged and rough as I used to be, but there's still a lot of work to be done...a lot of grinding and chipping...before the world will be able to recognize all that the Lord sees when He looks at me. After all, He sees me as I can be, sees my potential.

The grinding is uncomfortable, and the chipping hurts something awful at times; but all my squirming and complaining doesn't stay the Master Polisher's hand. And the promise that He knows exactly how much has to be removed, and where to direct the blows of His mallet, is sufficient to give me peace as I go through the process.

That smooth stone in my pocket isn't as beautiful as it will be someday. And I may not be beautiful now, either. But I, too, will be...someday.

Parable of The Table Lamp, the Teacup and the Ladder-back Chair

Ever since I was nine or ten years old I have been the household fixer and putter-together-of-new-stuff guy. In fact, my dad could hardly wait for me to become personally acquainted with Santa Claus so that I could be recruited as his assembly-elf. And, as you may know, once you have been so recruited you receive a life-time commission in the assembly and repair service.

As the big brother to two sisters, and later the daddy to three daughters, I became expert at untangling necklaces, repairing jewelry, unsticking some things and making other things stick. This is not something I learned from my dad. His philosophy was that he was successful at what he did for a living (he owned a respected Direct Mail Advertising company) and he was willing to pay others to do what they were good at. That included most household handyman chores.

I discovered, primarily as a result of necessity, I could mend and maintain things. As a new head of household with a growing family, I couldn't indulge Dad's philosophy of paying someone else to do things that needed to be done, so I gradually began to tackle them myself. To my delight I found that I could do a fairly good job of repairing, restoring and reclaiming all sorts and sizes of items that would have otherwise have been thrown out.

There was the antique table lamp that wasn't particularly attractive, and its only appeal was its age. It was almost in pieces, it wouldn't light, the cord—one of the old fabric-covered lamp cords—was frayed, with wires showing. However, I replaced the light sockets, tightened some screws, put in new wiring and transformed it to a thing of light—if not a thing of beauty.

There was the delicate porcelain teacup with the handle and a big piece broken out of one side. It was one of a small and undistinguished collection of bric-a-brac that came from Grandmother's house. Its value was purely sentimental...which, of course, renders many such articles priceless. A little bit of crazy glue expertly applied, and thoughtful placement on the shelf, turned just so, and it was restored as an attractive decorative accessory.

And then, there was the case of the ladder-back chair. It was weathered and gray, missing a rung and so rickety that I could hardly keep it together long enough to get it into the car. When I got it home, my loving wife asked, "How long do we have to have *that* in the house?" However, after I had refinished it, repaired the broken rung, re-glued it and put in a new cane seat, she changed her tune. She coyly informed me she had plans for that "cute" chair. That happens a lot now that I am the business of restoring and re-caning chairs and rockers.

The point of these three illustrations is this: All around us we can find multitudes of items, once useful, attractive and valuable, that have been discarded because they are broken, or have become dirty or tarnished with overuse or abuse. Their original worth has been lost, or is no longer apparent. They are disdained, ignored and eventually discarded.

That goes for people, too. We often tend to judge the value of people by their speech, by their appearance, by their current occupation. Because their evident qualities do not match our expectations or our personal standards, we are inclined to disdain, ignore and discard them.

It is a marvelous thing to realize that the Lord is in the business of maintaining, fixing and restoring people. There is no character so flawed, no life so blemished, no personality so bent, that He is unable to mend it and infuse it with a usefulness that exceeds its original condition. He delights in regenerating those who have been tossed onto the curb by society.

He seldom does this with His own hands, however. He sends selected agents to perform this miraculous restoration. He recruits you and me...when we're available...as His "fixers."

Parable of The Talents

"I'll bet that if you would mat and frame them, and put them out in shops, you could sell those." That's what I was once told by a professional artist and art teacher. She was in my office with some watercolors she wanted our printing firm to reproduce in a brochure. While waiting for some price information, she had looked around my office at some framed photographs of mine that I had put up to give a little personality to my work place.

"Your work reminds me of the photographs of G. Elliott Porter," she said. Since I had never heard of him, she went on to identify him as a very successful, well-known professional photographer who specialized in interesting outdoor shots. She even gave me a book of his, illustrated by many of his pictures. And, you know, he did seem to see things the way I do.

Selling my "work"...I liked the sound of that, so I made prints of some of my favorite photos, matted them and took them to a number of art and gift shops in the area. Each one told me the same thing. "Those are very nice. You should be able to sell a lot of them."

But nobody bought them. Not even one. I still have them...at least those that weren't finally given to family and friends as gifts.

Then I thought that maybe they didn't sell because a lot of people don't think of photographs as artwork. Perhaps pen and ink sketches done from some of my best photos would be more saleable. I carefully selected the subjects I thought were most appealing and did eight drawings—even made the negatives myself so that I could make a limited edition of artist prints. In addition to limited edition prints, I printed and packaged sets of note cards, and full-size prints suitable for framing or decoupage. I took them around to art and gift shops. Each one told me, "Those are very nice. You should be able to sell a lot of them."

But nobody bought them. They also make excellent gifts and remembrances to family and friends. (I still have a few cartons of them if you know anyone who would like a nice gift.)

Could it be that some other medium would be more saleable? Maybe pencil drawings? How about other types of subjects? "Those are very nice. You should be able to sell a lot ..." I've discovered that pencil drawings make excellent gifts, too.

I have written some "very nice" poetry, some of it inspired by photos, sketches and drawings. I've been told that I could probably get them published if I could find just the right company. I haven't pursued that idea, although I have copies of my poems available if you would like one to give to a friend. Original poems make outstanding gifts, don't you think?

I have been told that I have a "very nice" voice, and I sing every chance I get. I'm a lot like the maiden lady my dad told about, who, when asked about her matrimonial intentions, said, "If you don't want me, don't ask me." However, I don't often get asked back. Go figure.

Don't misunderstand me. This is not a "Poor, poor, pitiful me" story. My point is simply this: I have come to realize that we have each been given an absolutely staggering "software package" of abilities, talents and skills. They come with the program, like the many features included when you purchase a personal computer. It is our responsibility to discover them and be alert to opportunities to use them throughout our lives. Some few of us will be responsible for using these talents for the benefit and enjoyment of large numbers of people...others will be able to share with a few friends and acquaintances. Most often our greatest satisfaction will come from exercising these skills for our own enjoyment, or passing them on to our family and those dearest to us. After all, it isn't the size of the audience, or the amount of the paycheck that accurately measures the value of a talent, but whether it was used well, and as often as possible.

Parable of The Tigers and the Gnats

I once read that the famous missionary to Africa, Dr. David Livingstone, was asked by a well intentioned missionary society matron, "Dr. Livingstone, weren't you frightened by the lions and the tigers?" He reportedly responded, "On the contrary, madam, it wasn't the tigers that got us, it was the gnats!"

There's a chance the story is apocryphal, but I hope not. It is, after all, an insightful commentary on our everyday lives.

Most of us spend a great deal of time anticipating and protecting ourselves against the big threats—the lions and tigers, if you will—which occasionally occur. And it certainly is prudent to be as well prepared as possible to withstand potentially catastrophic events... to avoid life's disasters. We read about them daily, and see them graphically reported on the evening news.

Today it is possible—if money is no object—to be insured against any and all hazards. We can buy life, health, accident, fire, casualty, and malpractice insurance. Security services guard and protect our homes and businesses. SUV's, family cars mounted on truck chassis, provide a sense of security from the menace of angry and aggressive drivers. Only the foolhardy fail to take measures to defend themselves against the muggers, robbers, car-jackers and kidnappers that make up the lead stories in the news media each day.

And yet, in my most reflective moments, I have to admit that very few of us are ever closely affected by these major events of which we all seem to be so fearful. The truth is that the real problems that most of us must deal with each day are more likely to be the "gnats" of life, rather than the tigers.

We may lock our mental and physical gates against the greater terrors of life, but the gnats can come in through the cracks and keyholes. Isn't it usually the ants, or the chiggers, or the mosquitoes that spoil the most enjoyable outing? The tiny grains of grit that set the teeth on edge and ruin the enjoyment of the Southerner's favorite soul food, turnip greens? The pebble in the shoe...the mote in the eye...small things that can instantly turn a happy time into a trial?

We humans are an emotionally fragile and easily unsettled lot, aren't we? And don't think for a minute that the adversary isn't aware of that, and that he isn't prepared to use the gnats of life in some of his most devastating stratagems.

When you have spent your day annoyed and dispirited by a cloud of those tiny events and minor problems that seem to flood in on us at times, take heart. Imitate the attitude of the little lady whose pastor asked her to recite her favorite Bible verse. She answered emphatically, "Oh, pastor, I find great comfort in the verse that says, '...and it came to pass ...'."

Gnat bites aren't fatal, and the Lord provides a soothing balm for their nagging itch. Let Him take charge, and never again be anxious about the lions and the tigers...or the gnats, either.

Parable of Underwater Safety

Among the skills that had to be passed if one expected to make an "A" in the Drownproofing Course—officially, Survival Swimming—was the 50-Yard Underwater Swim. The instructions were clear enough: Take a deep breath, jump into the deep end of the pool, push off the wall, swim to the far end, touch the wall, and return to the point where you started. All underwater. Simple. Piece of cake.

Well...to quote a word-for-word translation of an old Spanish proverb, "From the saying to the doing, it makes quite a stretch." In other words, "Easier said than done." The underwater swim was a good example. However, with the right technique, it's easier than one might think.

The first half dozen or so swimmers to master each skill were expected to help the coach keep an eye on the rest of the students as they made their attempts. I had really enjoyed the Drownproofing course, passing the skills and often acting as one of those assistant coaches. The underwater swim found me at Coach Lanoue's side, watching as each swimmer attempted the submerged trip, ready to jump in at the first sign of trouble and pull the foundering one to safety.

We observed one after another, and pulled several out when they were in distress. My most vivid recollection of the experience, however, is of one of the stronger swimmers who had made the first leg of the circuit with good, strong strokes and pushed off for the return.

Before he had taken more than a couple of strokes, Coach Lanoue said, "Watch him. He's about to pass out." He said that he could tell if one was in trouble well before the swimmer himself knew it.

Sure enough, as we watched, the swimmer's strokes became more mechanical, even spasmodic, as he approached the end of the pool. He touched the wall, began to reach for the surface, and then just slid back under water...unconscious, but eyes still open. "Now!" Coach Lanoue ordered. We were in the water instantly and pulled him out before he even had a chance to cough or get a mouthful of water. He didn't even know he had passed out.

Later, Coach Lanoue told the class that he always watched each swimmer on the underwater swim and took no chances with one who couldn't make the whole length, pulling them out before they got into trouble. But he would allow the stronger, more determined swimmers to go to the limit of their endurance before he intervened, encouraging the self-confidence and self-reliance that resulted from the knowledge that they hade finished the course.

When we think we are in deep water and feel we can't keep going, it is well for us to be reminded that we have a Comforter watching from the side of the pool. One who recognizes the signs of distress; who knows the extent of our determination and ability; who is ready to send His messengers to us; who will let us get to the end of our resources; but One who will wait until exactly the right moment before He intervenes.

I have been pulled out of deep water many times, always at exactly the right time. I have also completed many tasks I thought were impossible for me, because I had the assurance that the Lord was watching from the sidelines, and would jump in and save me if I should need it.

The Psalmist wrote, "I have been a young man and now I am old, and I have never seen the righteous forsaken, nor his seed begging bread." It's amazing to realize that the Creator of the Universe enjoys nothing more than to be trusted to watch over us and provide for all our needs...to protect us from disaster, but to allow us enough freedom to make decisions that test the limits of our abilities. I find myself greatly comforted by the understanding that anywhere I go and in anything I do, at any time, He and His messengers are near, cheering me on...ready to dive in to help, protect and save me from all perils, and finally bring me safely to Himself.

Parable of **Persistence**

The Easter service was well-planned and preparations had been made. The music and the message had been coordinated, the choir and orchestra were thoroughly practiced. The musical focal point was an anthem combining the orchestra and choir, titled "The Lord Reigns!" When the weekly church bulletin arrived, however, it announced with authority a title that raised a lot of eyebrows: "The Lord Resigns!"

Now, it's true the Bible tells us that the Lord "shall not strive with man forever," but could He possibly get so tired of our selfishness and misbehavior that he would actually resign? I've thought about it, and I think that if I were in charge of things I would have resigned a long time ago. Do you suppose God might sometimes be tempted to walk out the door and leave a sinful world to itself, just to teach us a lesson?

One of my professors—we called him "the judge," because he taught a series of classes on business law—was discussing the legal concept of "acts of God" one day. It was his opinion that the phrase was poorly chosen, because, as he said, "I think God has better things to do than sit around and stir up storms, floods and other kinds of natural disasters." In fact, his theory was that God designed and built the universe like a perfectly engineered machine, gave it a kick-start, and then went off to tend to other matters more challenging to His omnipotence, leaving His new creation to run on its own.

The secular world observes with interest the cynicism and lack of enthusiasm of many self-proclaimed believers, and there is no wonder it concludes that God has already resigned...given up on us...gone fishing, out of His disappointment with mankind's performance. Who could blame Him?

There are some things I have come to understand about the Creator, though, and among them is this: The One Who originated the traits we associate with the highest levels of human character possesses them all in their most perfect form. And of all those characteristics, I believe the one for which I am most grateful is His divine persistence.

In His patience, He waits for us to hear Him and respond to His urging. However, it is the persistence of His actions upon us, within us and on our behalf that finally moves resistant, reluctant hearts to achieve His will for the lives of those who love Him.

He hasn't resigned...or left us to our own devices, but has assigned His Spirit to be with us while He has, as the angel proclaimed, gone ahead of us to the appointed meeting place. And as soon as everything is prepared He will call us, each in his or her own turn, to join Him.

When that time comes for each of us, my pastor, Greg DeLoach, suggested that the most appropriate funeral music isn't "Taps," signaling the end of day, but, rather, "Reveille," the traditional bugle call to rouse or waken, in recognition of the fact that we will be awakened by the Lord Himself and "raised to walk with Him in newness of life."

And, for those who persist...who live and remain in service until the End Time...perhaps the most suitable bugle call should be "Charge!" That might startle those attending a memorial service, but wouldn't that be a great tribute to the Persistence of a Saint?

Parable of Proper Etiquette

Allow me to introduce Buster...actually, Buster Kitten. He is the last (at least for the present) of a succession of cats that have taken residence with us over the past three and a half decades, and has put up with us the longest of them all. Buster is black with white toes, and sports a white cravat. He came to us as a kitten, the survivor of an accident, or perhaps the attack of one of his fellow creatures, that left a gaping gash in his neck. Our daughter heard his mournful meowings coming from the shrubbery outside her apartment in Winston Salem and rushed him to the vet for some emergency pet repairs.

Although his new "Mom" spent much of the time on the road as a member of a touring ballet company, Buster survived and thrived. Her landlord allowed no pets on the property, but our dancer somehow charmed him into keeping an eye on the tiny trespasser for her while she was traveling with the Company. When she moved back to Atlanta, of course, little Buster Kitten came, too, traveling in one of her fuzzy bedroom slippers. In keeping with family custom, when she moved on, Buster (no longer "Kitten") took up residence with us.

Buster comes with all the usual features, good and bad, that are part of the package when you become the property of a cat. He bathes himself, doesn't need to be entertained—in fact seldom can be bothered—doesn't make a lot of noise...at least, not often. On the down side, there is the need to constantly clean up hair balls and things knocked onto the floor and broken...repair or replace wallpaper, upholstery, etc., that have been victimized by his claws...put into the rag bag clothes that have been turned to terrycloth by his instinctive kneading reflex on those rare occasions when he favors your lap with a visit. And, of course, his periodic, irresistible urge to deliver "P"-mail to several key message centers around the house.

Although our good will is often pushed to the limit, however, his good traits (not to mention the fact that by now he is becoming quite elderly and "we probably won't have to put up with him much longer") outweigh the bad, and we resist the temptation to perform unspeakable acts of vengeance on him for his selfish indulgences.

After all, Buster does show signs of an awareness of proper feline etiquette. One of the most interesting is in the act of hygiene following his trips to the litter box. If you've ever watched this kitty ritual you know that it typically consists of a cat depositing his gift in the middle of the litter box, then systematically covering it with the litter material.

Buster's approach to this instinctive behavior, however, demonstrates his distaste for such an unsanitary activity. When he has completed his period of meditation, Buster carefully checks to see if the product of his effort is properly placed in the litter, then he steps out of the box onto the clean bathroom floor and proceeds to rub his paws vigorously on the floor in the customary digging motion. After six of eight strokes he will return to the litter box to see if the offering has been covered. Of course, it hasn't. He will repeat this action two or three more times, then, as if deciding it was all a waste of time anyway, go on to more useful pursuits.

Buster's instincts are good; his execution is correct; however, his application is flawed. I've thought of submitting this ritual to "America's Funniest Home Videos," but I don't know how well animal potty humor will go over there.

Each of us has some ways in which we are like Buster and the litter box. We all have those particular areas where we know what we ought to do...we know how things should be done...we know there's no use trying to get out of doing them. But we want to do them in an easier...or faster...or less costly...or more convenient way. So we follow the proper motions, but in the way we *want*, instead of the way we *should*. In one way or another we have the same result as Buster: something unpleasant and distasteful is left for someone else to cover up for us.

Do you suppose that's the way God looks at our attitude toward sin? We know what we ought to do and how we should do it, but we decide to leave it undone, or done halfway, or done in a way that is altogether wrong. Then we walk blithely away, thinking we've done all that could be done "under the circumstances."

I believe that Jesus not only has covered our litter time and time again, but has emptied the litter box once and for all. The only thing He expects of us is to trust Him completely, the way Buster trusts those of us he thinks of as his pets and who provide for him.

Parable of The Cats

Only one of our feline foster kittens came from a normal chain of events. That was Mittens, pick of the litter of the furry lady of the evening up the street who yielded to the charms of a ne'er-do-well knave of a cat who was never identified. Mittens continued the chain of females—I was the only male in the house for a very long time.

We decided to let little Mittens experience the wonders of intimate relationships with creatures of her own kind, so weren't too surprised when she began to put on a little weight during her first summer at our house. Our girls were able to see her new kittens and how she took care of them, at one point setting up a nest in the inner confines of the old pump organ in the den. However, one litter was enough to try to get rid of, and we got her "heater" fixed.

Mittens was sweet and lovable, but unfortunately cashed in her nine lives while our girls were still relatively young. I'll always remember when our daughter Lauri, after we had given Mittens a proper burial in the back woods, asked me if she would see Mittens in heaven. This was, I think, the first time the reality of death struck home to any of our children, and I was concerned about the best way to teach them how a loving God could possibly allow the passing of such a beloved pet.

I told her, "Honey, all I know is what the Bible says about heaven for you and me. It tells us that heaven is a lovely place where God lives, and that when we get there we will have no sorrow, no sadness, no pain, no regret. There will be no tears there. Only joy and beauty and love. If that is true, and I truly believe it is, then I can promise you this: If it will take having Mittens with you there for you to be happy, then God will see to it that Mittens and you will be together."

Then along came Al, a gray tramp of a tabby cat. He must have seen the mysterious mark that hobos and other strays leave indicating where a free meal can be had with a minimum of effort, because one day he jumped up on the ledge outside the open kitchen window and introduced himself. "AL!", he said. Or, at least that was what it sounded like, so we assumed that was his name...and thus it became.

Somewhere along the line Al's manhood had been tampered with, leaving him, like Ferdinand the Bull, more inclined toward naps and silent meditation than to wild nights out with the boys. When the cat carousals got too rowdy the others would chase him home, and, without the extra weight of his pilfered plumbing, he could jump high onto the ledge outside the living room windows. "Al! Al!," he would announce, and wait for us to let him in through the screen.

Al relied too heavily on his relationship to me as the only other male in the family, however. One dark day he disgraced himself in one of my wife's favorite pieces of luggage, and his sojourn with us was over. I regret being the one who had to betray him into the hands of the Humane Society. I'll always remember hearing him hopefully introducing himself to the folks there. "Al! Al!" Sorry, Al, but even between guys certain niceties are expected; proper etiquette forbids marking your territory on Mama's stuff. Goodbye, Al, old friend.

Some of the best of life's lessons can be learned from pets. We can learn about the origin of life, and that there is a natural end that need not be feared if life's priorities have been heeded. We learn about the importance of responding to what is expected of us, and that there are penalties for falling short of those expectations. We learn that very little in life is permanent, and that after every loss there is the comfort of many cherished memories that warm the heart and soothe the tender spirit. Having been owned by a cat can do that.

Parable of The Cats—Part 2

One thing seems to be consistent with people who have pets. No matter what kind of experience one has had with a pet, it seems that once you've been owned by one, you're hooked. I guess that's especially true with cats—at least it has been with our family.

I've been told that guys are supposed to prefer owning dogs to being owned by cats. However, with me it was something more practical than sentimental. Cats take care of themselves. They learn while still kittens to use the litter box. They wash themselves. They will not overeat. They entertain themselves most of the time and are not so emotionally needy. Hey, that's my kind of pet...a low-maintenance best friend. (At least in theory, which I may want to debate some other time.)

It all started innocently enough with Mittens; then there were Al, Minominop and Zero.

I've already related the tales (pun intended, of course) of Mittens and Al, and their separate and disparate departures.

Shortly after Al's deportation and Mittens' demise, our daughter Lauri spent a summer in New York, studying with the Joffery Ballet. She somehow found herself attached to a stray gray New York City kitten which she named Minominop. She got the name from a popular song that was used by the Muppets as background for one of their puppet sketches.

She brought Minop home on the airplane, perched on a pile of Kleenex and hidden inside her pocketbook. The flight attendants were obviously deaf, dumb and blind to allow her aboard. I will have to say, though, that Minop was extremely well mannered and discreet, leaving very little mess and only a slight kitten aroma (most of which went away with time) in what I am told was a fairly expensive pocketbook.

As with most pets brought home by our children, when Lauri went back to New York for three years, Minop became ours to take care of. In time she took her place beside Mittens under the leaves, poison ivy and pine straw in the far reaches of the back yard..

Now Zero was another matter. He was a foster cat in the most common use of the term. He belonged to the family next door, but eschewed the handling and carrying around and chasing that was part of living with small children, so he took up residence with us. I understand that his name came from the fact that he was absolutely worthless. He was aptly named.

Zero ate at our house, slept at our house, and generally made our home his. He wasn't a young cat...and something of a cat-curmudgeon...but he and I got along well. Zero wasn't much for etiquette at his age, but since he kept to himself no one noticed. That was how he came to fit in so well with the family. So much so, in fact, that when we made plans to move, his real family said it would be a kindness to him (and, I suspect, to them as well) if we moved him with us. That's how Zero came with us to Marietta in his latter years, and came to be the first occupant of our new back woods memorial plot.

So that's pretty much how we came to be cat people. I've observed the wisdom of cats, in choosing just the right time to seek out a comfortable lap, but knowing when to play it cool and stay aloof. Cats keep their opinions to themselves most of the time, but when the time comes to make their feelings known, they don't hold back. They're not spiteful or mean...and on those rare occasions when they show a fit of pique, they get it out of their systems quickly and everything immediately returns to normal. Things are never so serious that cats can't take a nap; and when suddenly awakened they can jump to the top of the china cabinet in one motion, instantly alert. Yep, I've learned a lot from cats. I'm certain I'll learn more. I'll let you know.

Parable of A Summer's Lightning

Our fears are a powerful force in our lives, and can lead us to do strange and unexpected things. There has been a lot written about the ignorance, superstition and fear that was prevalent during the Dark Ages. Much misery and pain, countless acts of cruelty resulted from irrational attempts to deal with anything and anyone feared as a threat to the health or well-being of individuals, communities or whole regions.

There is a whole area of Psychology dealing with phobias, recognizing their power over certain susceptible people. A phobia is "A persistent, abnormal or illogical fear of a thing or situation." A shorter definition is "An irrational fear."

What is the difference between a rational fear and an irrational fear? I suppose that depends on one's point of reference. I am afraid of poisonous snakes—can't stand them. My wife, on the other hand will gladly pound to dust any reptile larger than an earthworm. She is a lot like the club-bearing female in the comic strip "B.C.," who, when she sees a snake in the cartoon's first frame, shouts, "SERPENT!" and there follow three frames of "WHAM! WHAM! WHAM!" as she pulverizes the hapless creature. THAT is a phobia.

A friend whose teen-age son had a nervous breakdown asked the Child Psychologist, "What problems can a teen-ager have that are real enough to cause a breakdown?" The doctor answered, "If the problems are real to him, then they are REAL." That's true, whether or not they are illogical or irrational.

When I was a small boy, I had two overwhelming phobias. One was being in deep water. I have written about learning to overcome that fear. The other one—one that I understand is quite common in small children—was the fear of lightning...or, to be more exact, the clap of thunder that almost always followed a flash of lightning. The summer thunderstorms that are so common in our part of the country were an absolute terror to me.

My dad had his own way of helping me deal with my fear. One summer evening, during a typical Georgia thunderstorm, Dad came into my bedroom to find me on my bed with the pillow over my head, crying in fright. He picked me up and held me a minute, then said, "Come on, let's go out and see what you're afraid of." Only his firm, Daddy-hug made it possible for me to go outside...of course, it also made it impossible for me to resist the dreaded trek.

Dad took me into our back yard, and the two of us lay on our backs with me closely snuggled next to his side, his right arm holding me close. There was no rain. Only the warm gusts of humid wind with the smell of the promise of rain. The sky was boiling with clouds, highlighted with the constant flashing of heat lightning, followed at intervals by the thunder which varied from rambling, unhappy grumbling to outrageous crashes that shook the earth.

As the sky would flash, Dad would give me a squeeze and say, "Now listen for the thunder. Here it comes...WOW! Wasn't that something? Here comes another one...wait...MAN! that was a beauty. God really knows how to put on a fireworks display, doesn't He?"

Ever since that night, I have loved thunderstorms. But that wasn't the only victory of that experience. I learned that I could count on Dad to be by my side to help me deal with anything that threatened me. Even when I discovered that he wasn't invincible...that he made mistakes...I found great comfort in the knowledge that my Dad was nearby.

More important, I learned that he was demonstrating the love of his God, Who, whenever I am faced with anything that I dread or fear—whether real or irrational—will always remain by my side. The One in charge of the summer lightning has everything under control, after all.

Parable of A Bumper Sticker Philosophy

Someone (and I don't think it was me—although, like many people, I sometimes hide what I believe to be original thoughts and sayings behind "They say...") once said, "We all need a philosophy of life that could fit on a bumper sticker." In other words, we can't hope to live a focused life or expect to achieve worthy goals if we don't understand what those goals are well enough to express them clearly and concisely to others.

That is not to say that, just because some smart aleck, malcontent or irresponsible nitwit has put a one-liner or wise crack on a sticker, the thought so proclaimed deserves to be taken seriously. On the other hand, I have gotten many a chuckle and not a few morsels for thought from those punchy and pungent literary miniatures.

Sometimes the statements are obnoxious, repulsive and even vulgar; other times they are vapid, banal and inane. (I love those words. And besides, they give different colors to the words "ugly" and "stupid," which are the words I would probably use on a bumper sticker.) Not too long ago, I saw one whiney and pitiful message that went, "Why this? Why here? Why now? Why ME?" Soon after that I read this complaining variation, "Anything but this! Anywhere but here! Anytime but now! Anyone but ME!" Come on, you people! Give me a break!

I used to be an Optimist. Don't misunderstand me—I'm still optimistic, but I once belonged to the civic club known as Optimists International. I like the Optimist Creed, which begins, "Promise yourself: To be so strong that nothing can disturb your peace of mind. To talk health, happiness and prosperity to every person you meet. To give every living creature you meet a smile. To make all your friends feel that there is something good in them." I'm not sure that is the correct order...and maybe I've messed up the wording... and I can't remember the rest of it. I do know, though, that Creed is an excellent example of an optimistic and inspiring philosophy of life. Unfortunately, you can't reduce that to a statement on a bumper sticker.

Over the years I have seen several of these succinct, pithy commentaries that I would be willing to have represent my life philosophy. One of them was the theme of an inspirational message that, as I understand it, was given by a famous football coach to his players and their supporters. He had banners and hand-out cards printed with this cryptic message: A^3–0. He challenged them to make this their personal and team motto. He told them it stood for "Anything, Anywhere, Anytime...Bar Nothing!"

That's a far cry from the grumbling and self-indulgent message of the stickers mentioned earlier, isn't it? And, as mottoes go, it demonstrates an attitude that is a key element in the fulfillment of a productive and satisfying life. It represents a determination to face obstacles and difficulties head-on, without exception, with the expectation of ultimate success.

Isn't that, after all, what the Creator had in mind for us? With the full knowledge that we have neither the strength, power nor wisdom to deal with these experiences on our own, we can know, nonetheless, that He has empowered those of us who trust Him to face all things, in every place, regardless of time, without exception. What a bumper sticker philosophy for today: A^3–0.

Parable of The Devil Dog

I have written about Cody, the white and tan mostly English Setter, mostly puppy, who came to live with our family. He was obviously undernourished and was uneasy and skittish around people. I learned later that was most likely because the teenagers in the neighborhood had teased and tormented him when he first appeared in the subdivision where we lived.

I have also written about some of the life lessons I learned while being his best friend. I learned something about leadership and followship...about patience and grace. And also about trust and being trustworthy.

We took Cody in as our foster-puppy because our daughter was working after school for a veterinarian at the time and convinced us that she would be responsible for taking care of him. However, when she moved into a "no pets" apartment, you could say that I lost a teenage daughter and gained a teenage (in dog years) canine.

Cody's likes and needs were fairly simple. Food, with the occasional table-scrap treat...water, preferably fresh, but an open, unattended toilet would do...a few kind words, preceded or followed by "Cody"...a friendly skritch behind the ears, or gentle thump on the side...he didn't ask for or expect much.

Of course, he did need to be taken out two or three times a day, so he could check up on the neighborhood. Rain or shine, windy or calm, snow storm or dust storm...he expected to be taken out morning, mid-day and night to deposit his doggy tokens and check his "P-mail."

My morning ritual called for taking Cody in a different one of the three possible directions from our street each day. We could go straight ahead, to the right or to the left at the cross street. Was variety in our daily walk important to a dog? I don't know. But it helped to make it more interesting for me, and therefore, helped it seem a little less like the chore it was.

There was one period, however, that it was not a good choice to take the left turn at the intersection. The reason was that one of our neighbors had a big black dog of unclear breed, but of quite clear animosity toward white dogs, and their humans, that happened into his domain. Somehow, this "devil" dog's owner didn't feel compelled to abide by the county's leash laws, and allowed him to run free while "doing his business."

When Cody and I would turn left and walk about thirty yards up the street, we would hear the threatening barking begin, and the devil dog would come charging up, with teeth bared and hair bristling, ready to tear us both to shreds. At first, Cody, already overwhelmed with deep psychological problems and feelings of inadequacy, would tuck his tail and cower behind me—as if suggesting to the devil dog that I might be a better offering than he would.

His aggressive and menacing behavior notwithstanding, the devil dog had apparently had some exposure to obedience training, because I discovered an effective way to stop him was to look steadily at him and firmly shout "NO!" When I did that, he would come to a screeching halt, and, with a few grudging growls, let us pass. After a few such encounters, I noticed that Cody no longer paid even the least attention to the devil dog. He seemed to sense that I had everything under control and he had nothing to worry about.

What a lesson to me! In my life I've had many occasions when the devil dogs have come charging, challenging my passage, threatening horrible consequences if I didn't turn back. But I have assurance that I belong to the One Who can repel any adversary with the authority of His "NO!" Like Cody, I can continue in confidence, because I belong to the One with power over the strategies and tactics of the one who brings evil, misery and discord to the world around me.

Parable of The Signal Light

Our family has always been one of those boisterous, lovey, huggy families. That may have been caused by my mother's overcompensation for what she felt she missed in her childhood. She told me many times that she couldn't remember a time that her parents showed any outward sign of affection—either between themselves or towards their children. She and her sister and two brothers knew they were loved, but only by intuition, not because the words were ever spoken.

So, for as long as I can remember, love in our family has been a contact sport, demonstrated in a vast variety of ways. Our hellos and goodbyes have always been noteworthy, the stuff of legend among newcomers to the family, often taking more time and energy than the activity for which we had come together. My sister once said that we were the kind of family that would gather on the front porch and all wave goodbye when one of us would go down to the corner for a loaf of bread. We can put on quite a show sometimes.

One of our parting rituals had its beginning from visits every couple of weeks, and on most of the holidays, to my grandparents' house in the West End section of Atlanta. When the time came we would all pile in the car to leave, and Ma-ma and "Podnuh" (that's Southern for "Partner," as my dad's step-father liked to be called) would stand on the little front porch and wave us out of sight. As we would go around the corner, Ma-ma would reach inside and blink the porch lights three times..."I Love You!" So began a family tradition we still practice today.

With that in mind, I've found it interesting to recall Dad's experience in the Navy during World War II. After completing boot camp he was assigned to signal school. He learned to be proficient with signal flags, and sending and receiving Morse Code using the telegraph key and the signal light. You have probably seen sailors using the signal light—a searchlight with what looks like a Venetian blind attached to the front of it. The signalman sends messages by manipulating the vanes to cover and uncover the light in the long and short flashes of the code.

Dad served as one of the two Navy signalmen on the liberty ship USS Dwight W. Morrow. Although they took turns on Signal Watch, the captain and crew distinguished between them by calling Dad "Flags" and his counterpart "Sparks." Although they were both experienced with all the signaling media, the captain usually called on Dad...or Flags...when he needed quick and accurate blinker sending and receiving, especially in port. Dad was really good with the signal light. In fact, Dad was good at just about everything he put his hand to.

In January of 1983, Dad had by far the most serious of his four heart attacks. His doctor said that approximately 85% of the heart muscle was destroyed, and that if he survived he would never be able to get out of bed again. He held on for nearly 24 hours—for most of which he was conscious and able to communicate. We were certain he was trying to stay with us long enough for my sister to get back to Georgia from her home in California. At one point he told my mother, "I've been fighting deadlines all my life, but I don't think I'm going to make this one."

And he didn't. But that's not the point of this parable.

For most of the last twenty-five years of his life, Dad was involved in a kind of Lay ministry, preaching evangelistic messages on occasion and teaching Lay Evangelism Schools to show Christians how to talk to others about Christ without embarrassment. His approach was to simply ask, "Tell me, do you know Jesus?" He said he had never had anyone take offense when approached with that question. Whatever their answer, he had an opening to share what Jesus meant to him.

While Dad was lying in the Cardiac Intensive Care Unit, he had conversations with anyone who happened to be around him when he was conscious. The last words anyone heard him speak were to the nurse attending him about an hour before he died. He was on his stomach and turned his head to see who was beside him. When he saw the nurse, he asked, "Honey, do you know Jesus?" She answered, "Yes, sir, I sure do." His response was, "I'll see you up there, then, won't I?" She replied, "Yes, sir, I'll be up there... and I know you will." His last words were directed toward bringing someone else into the Kingdom with him.

Within an hour of those words, we were all called into the room as it was clear that his heart was at last winding down. We silently watched as his breathing slowed and stopped, and as the line on the heart monitor flickered another time or two and surrendered into a straight line traversing the screen. And our hearts wanted to stop, too.

As the family gathered again out in the hall, it happened that a severe thunderstorm came across metropolitan Atlanta and barreled through Lawrenceville, buffeting cars and houses, shaking trees and rattling power poles. That shaking and rattling caused a number of power surges—three, in fact. As we stood there in that hall, the lights blinked three times. "I Love You!" We looked at each other and began to laugh and cry at the same time. "Well, he's just letting us know that he made it home all right," my sister said.

Does God send thunderstorms to make His children know that He has things under control? I don't have any trouble believing that, but that's not the point of this parable, either. The point is this: God has given us the ability to see in every experience an indication that He knows what is happening in our lives. He has given us the ability to bank those experiences for withdrawal later, when we need help to cope with difficult times. For our family it was the experience of the blinking light. What is it for you?

Parable of The Well-Chosen Word

It only happened once that I can remember. I had only been driving for a few months, and Mom was letting me drive to school. She was in the front seat with me, and two of my friends, Billy and C.B., were in the back. As I made the turn onto North Fulton Drive, I mismanaged the clutch and roughly introduced second gear to the drive shaft, which responded with an unfriendly growl and grinding of teeth.

Embarrassed in front of my friends, and upset with myself for the inept demonstration, I muttered—not entirely to myself—"Da—!" "What did you say?" Mom asked sharply—not entirely amused. Dutifully keeping my eyes on the street ahead, "I said 'Dang!'," I told her, trying to pronounce the verbal stand-in as much like "Da—!" as possible.

My two chums snorkled (not as in scuba diving—it's just the closest I can come to the sound they made...a cross between a snort and a chuckle) in the back seat. Mom probably would have, too, if it wouldn't have spoiled a "teachable moment." She was a cool mom, though, and didn't say anything about the incident. To the best of my knowledge she never heard me say another dirty word. I used them...but I was careful not to let her hear me.

Mom was a real stickler for polite euphemisms. An English teacher she admired impressed her with the idea that vulgar language was a sign of a lack of intelligence, and that certain words were less gracious and cultured sounding than others. So, all our lives "stinks" was out..."smells" was in; "liar" was out..."story-teller" was in; "butt", definitely out..."bottom," in; "belly" bad..."tummy" or "stomach" good; and so on, and so on.

However, my polite language was reserved for public application, with family and strangers, including all adults. Among my male friends and peers, I utilized a vocabulary and form of expression that could curl your hair, and would likely guarantee me my own reality TV show by today's standards. Mind you, it wasn't rude, malicious or spiteful; just coarse and vulgar...not suitable for polite conversation, and never around ladies. (I can't tell you how appalled I was to realize that girls used some of the same language.) I consistently and freely used profanity around my high school chums and college fraternity brothers, though.

When I was a college freshman, I became the teacher of a Sunday School class of thirteen-year-old boys, and that all changed. I thought, "What if one of those boys heard the way I talk around the fraternity house? What kind of a witness would that be?" That was the day I made up my mind to stop using any language I would have to apologize for. And I did.

It was during that period of adjustment that I made an interesting observation. People seldom used a foul word because the word itself had any real significance. We can't damn anyone, or send them to hell. Why say words for things we would never put into our mouths?

Then I reasoned, if it isn't the words themselves, but rather the manner in which they are uttered that matters, why not use words that won't offend others? A rousing "Dadgummit!" is just as effective as a "Damn!" or a "Hell!" and you don't have to apologize. Charlie Brown's "Drat!"...Pogo Possum's "Frammidge!", or my favorite, "Rowrbazzle!" pronounced sincerely and with authority are entirely as effective as any of the common oaths used today. That way, one can avoid explaining why it's all right for Daddies to say those words, but not for their kids.

Always keep in mind there may be someone whose respect you value within earshot.

Finally, remember that the tongue can exert leverage on the mind. If I can control my tongue, I can control my mind and thoughts, making them acceptable to the One Who hears the words spoken in my heart. As David said, "Set a guard over my mouth, O Lord." (Psalm 141:3)

Parable of Things Remembered

Among the multitude of scientific developments that have occurred in recent years is one that I think is quite remarkable. Well...there are actually many that I find remarkable, but this one is especially so. You have probably seen it advertised. It is a kind of plastic material that is said to have "memory."

By memory they mean that no matter how much it is dented or deformed it will return to its original shape. I have seen the ads on television. A car bumper made of this material is assaulted by sledge hammers, backed into objects...even crashed into by other cars. No matter how serious the damage appears, after a few seconds the bumper is observed to slowly resume its form, as if some unseen hands were at work.

I prefer to think of memory in its more conventional usage, however. Although there is a definite advantage to having materials capable of returning to their intended state, I don't think that is the purpose of human memory. Rather, our memories are intended to provide us with a frame of reference by which to measure and evaluate our current situations and experiences.

Some of my earliest memories have to do with a duplex in Decatur, Georgia. My mother had a photograph taken of me standing in one of the windows in just a diaper, pressing my face against the window screen. I couldn't have been much over a year old, but I remember that scene, except seen from the inside, looking out. I remember playing with other children in the sandy yard—there wasn't any grass—and playing hide-and-seek behind scraggly shrubbery.

I remember standing at attention in the dimly lighted living-room next to my brother, Freddy, our hands over our hearts, as the radio station signed off for the day by playing the National Anthem—then running upstairs to get into bed. I remember waking in the mornings to the mooing of cows in the pasture behind that duplex—if I recall correctly, there was a dairy there, even if we were just a few blocks from Decatur's town square.

As pleasant as those recollections are, I don't have any desire or expectation that the memory of them should serve to bring them back. They are like the push-pins we stick into a travel map, indicating the route we followed to get us where we are. Like the slides in a family vacation show, their purpose is merely to remind me of the experiences that, taken together, served to mold and shape me into who I have become.

In recent years, there has been another aspect of memory that I have come to appreciate. During times of difficulty with my business, especially the period of time which I delicately refer to as "being available for immediate employment," a good memory has proved to be one of my most valued gifts. Without a good memory, I would have experienced numerous periods of despair, as financial needs began to press in and resources rapidly evaporated.

Whenever I have been tempted to worry or be anxious, my heroic memory would spring into action, flashing vivid pictures on the projection screen inside my forehead...slide after slide recalling occasions when the Lord provided what was needed—always just in time, and in just the right amount...never too soon or too late, and neither more nor less than it took to solve the immediate problem. Like manna in the wilderness...enough for each day...one day at a time.

No, the Creator's gift of memory isn't planned as a means of returning things to the way they were in some fondly—if inaccurately—recalled past event; but rather to give us a frame of reference for facing the present, as well as the future. Memory is like a rear-view mirror that makes it possible for us to go ahead with confidence, because we can see from where we have come, and how the Lord has faithfully provided for us time and time again. Precious memories.

Parable of Traveling with Mom

I heard once that one of the ten most important inventions in history was the flanged wheel. Some of the others I knew about, of course, like the lever, the inclined plane, and the basic wheel; but the flanged wheel? Well, it seems that the flanged wheel is what makes it possible for a vehicle to run on a track, making rail transportation possible. It was the flanged wheel, running on steel rails that carried the Industrial Revolution into modern times.

Another vehicle made possible by the flanged wheel was the streetcar. Some of my most vivid childhood memories include riding the streetcar from our end of the line at the East Lake Country Club to the other end of the line at what is now known as Underground Atlanta. To a small boy, that was a remarkable adventure.

The adventure began with me in Sunday clothes, and Mom dressed like all respectable Southern ladies of her day, down to the hat, gloves, high heels and stockings—with seams perfectly straight, of course. We would walk the two or three blocks to the "car line" and wait for the street car to arrive.

If our timing was right, we would get there in time for me to watch the conductor make the transformation that would convert the East-bound car into the West-bound car. He would walk from one end of the car to the other, toggling the backs of the bench seats so they faced in the opposite direction, then lift the control handle from the drive panel on the "old" front end and move it to the "new" front end. Finally, after putting on the greasy motorman's gloves, he would pull down the trolley pole from the "old" rear end and raise the trolley pole to contact the power wires on the "new" rear end. After the marvelous metamorphosis was complete, he would climb aboard and announce that we were ready to head downtown.

Riding that streetcar, with the exotic rhythm in the clatter of its wheels as it rolled through woods, over bridges, through back yards and alongside roadways was always a thrilling experience, brimming with mystery and intrigue, unmatched by anything short of a journey on the Trans-India Railway from Bombay to Calcutta. At least in the imagination of a small boy.

I remember walking hand-in-hand from Rich's Department Store to Davison-Paxon, now Macy's—both long gone from downtown Atlanta—and back again...with stops at all the shops in between. I must have been worn out—we both must have been—after all that walking, but I don't remember that. Only the memory of a little boy and his Mommy exploring the big city. Then the wondrous streetcar/jungle railway ride home.

I have recalled those images many times over the years, but especially so recently as I looked down on my mother, by then almost 89 years on this earth. After a massive stroke, she lay there, unconscious and unresponsive, with heart racing and her respiration rapid, but shallow. The doctor said that her body was responding like that of a runner approaching the end of a marathon race, and that soon it would reach the end of its resources and give out.

Well, she was ready to go—she has had her bags packed and has been waiting...sometimes not so patiently...for the Lord to call her home for quite a while now. I felt as if we were standing on the platform with her, waiting for that last streetcar to take her to the end of the line. Eager to see her on her way to the place she had been dreaming of for such a long time, but reluctant to face the loss we were to experience upon her departure.

As the end drew nearer, family and church friends were gathered around her bed, singing her favorite hymns and praying. Richelieu, the Liberian seminary student who called her "Grandmother," prayed an eloquent prayer and concluded by saying, "... Lord, we don't want to let Grandmother go, but we pray that You will help us lift her up to You with open hands ..." At that moment, Mom's eyes opened for the first time since her stroke, and her breathing became regular and even. Those who noticed the change began to sing "Praise God from Whom All Blessings Flow," and as the song was concluded, her eyes slowly closed, her breathing stopped, and she was gone.

In the little boy part of my imagination, I can picture her running hard to catch the streetcar, climbing aboard, leaning back in relief and finally relaxing as the exotic clatter of the flanged wheels on the steel rails carries her rhythmically on to adventures that even a little boy can't possibly imagine.

Her little boy can't go with her this time—at least not yet. He just stands on the curb at the car-stop waving until she's out of sight.

Parable of The Cow Paths

It's one of the most pleasant and peaceful places I've ever been. And in the Fall, when the leaves in the Smokey Mountains National Park are at their peak, Cade's Cove is among the most beautiful and picturesque spots one could ever hope to visit. It is also an excellent place to study and reflect on the peculiarities of human nature.

By far the best way to enjoy the scenery and atmosphere of the Cove is to turn off the radio...or CD player, or whatever other kind of noisemaker you have in your car...turn off the air conditioner, and roll down the windows. Then put your car in Low and let it slowly mosey around the 11-mile loop road as you soak up the luxurious quietude of the small, rustic valley that once supported a thriving pioneer community.

And, Oh! the sounds you'll hear. There are birds...song birds and hunters. There are the whirring, wing-assisted jumps of grasshoppers in the breeze-brushed pasture. You can hear from time to time the crystal clatter of the small streams, stumbling across the smoothed stones that make up their beds as they stretch down from the hills and join together to run down the center of the Cove, nourishing it and making life possible. You'll hear cattle and horses calling from field to field, and the occasional unidentified creature's muffled messages from the dense stands of trees that border the Cove. And in between there's an impressive quietness.

On the other hand, there is the disagreeable grumble of certain tourists' cars as they come around the loop road as rapidly as they can, passing those of us who want to enjoy and truly experience the charm of this magical place. They would be comical, if they weren't so pitiful, with their windows rolled up to keep out the smell of livestock, and the invasion of the occasional insect...their air conditioners cranked up full blast...and their stereo systems pounding the air for a hundred yards in all directions, with bass speakers capable of stampeding cattle, of leaving bruises on bystanders and turning soft tissue into jelly. They don't stop or slow down if they can help it, looking quickly from side to side as they breeze through, hindered only by "jerks" like me who poke along, soaking in every little detail. They're going to enjoy Nature if it kills them, by golly... just so it doesn't take too long. But enough about my pet peeves.

As one stands by one of the snake rail fences and looks across the flat floor of the Cove, one of the interesting sights is that of the numerous well-worn paths meandering aimlessly from place to place, sometimes several running almost side-by-side, then fanning out only to converge again without any apparent rhyme or reason. Each path indicates the favorite route of one or more of the long-suffering cows as they go about their rounds day after day, each with his or her own independent idea of the ideal way to get there. They stubbornly refuse to accept the possibility that another path might also serve their transportation needs.

Humans are God's creatures, too, and suffer from the same affliction as the cows. We also have our cow paths. If you doubt that, just look at the layout of the streets and boulevards in a city like

Atlanta. Many of them are merely rambling cow paths, long since paved over.

More to be avoided, however, are the wandering cow paths of the mind. These are the long held beliefs and prejudices, the patterns of thought and argument that have been handed down for so long that they are accepted without question—and no one knows where they came from. We are not bound to follow those mental trails evermore, although many choose to do so.

We are independent spirits, called to be courageous mental adventurers; to confidently keep to well-reasoned courses of thought at times, but to fearlessly launch out across untracked territory when circumstances demand it, in search of wisdom and truths that resonate within us.

Parable of A House Deserted

You can still see them, scattered through the South's rural landscape. The familiarity of that scene was probably the reason the photograph of the deserted sharecropper's house caught my attention. It was a typical setting, out in the middle of more or less cultivated farm land, with an old tree or two to provide a little shelter from the withering winter winds and the oppressive summer sun.

Most of the time these houses appear isolated and forlorn, standing at the end of overgrown, deeply rutted dirt and gravel roads that, in simpler times, provided the only umbilical to civilization. More recently there might be the wire-strung poles bringing the added marvel of electricity to help ease the burden of the workers living there—or, perhaps, make it possible to start work earlier and continue working later with the hope of thereby making ends meet.

Often these four-walled carcasses are seen to be in the process of being conquered by the weeds and wild vegetation their former tenants fought so hard to defeat while eking out a living from the uncooperative red clay. It isn't uncommon to see them overgrown with wild plum or blackberry thickets...or the Southern trademark of a green counterpane of Kudzu.

The tin roofs are rusted, and sometimes rumpled at the edges by the disrespectful wind. The windows are usually cracked and broken...shutters and doors hang askew. The roof beams, and floor joists on their piles of field stones, are sagging...finally beginning to give in to the ultimately irresistible tug of gravity.

Countless families of sharecroppers found their homes in houses just like the one in the photograph. Sharecropping was a kinder, gentler generation's substitute for the shameful and often savage institution of slavery. The sharecropper was an independent businessman, perhaps, performing a service that was important for the nation's economy. But he often found himself in a cycle that kept him, and generations of his family, bound to the little parcel of land belonging to his landlord, with little hope of escaping to the status of property owners.

As with most occupations of that age requiring physical labor, sharecropping was difficult work, yielding little reward and often taking the efforts of family members of all ages to eke out a meager subsistence from the stubborn red dirt. The most aggressive and persistent struggle was barely enough to afford the most serious of needs—there were few niceties...luxuries didn't even exist in the sharecropper's vocabulary.

The days were hard, and often there was little to show for the most difficult day's labor. It's really no surprise that many were physically and emotionally ground to dust under the unbearable burden of the sharecroppers' lot. Countless masses of them packed up and moved with their families to the cities, where there was the promise of more generous return for their exertions. And these melancholy monuments to a bygone time are all that mark their passing.

In many ways, though, these deserted wooden relics of a less prosperous past, are at the same time a reason for encouragement to each one who works hard to find his or her way in this world. True, some of the former occupants of these structures went in search of a better life and never found it—they and their successors are still in comparable quarters some place else...still scratching unsuccessfully to make their way.

However, these abandoned houses offer hope to those seeking to provide a more abundant life for their families. They are vivid memorials to those not willing to stay bound as slaves to the soil, but who were able to move on to seek greater opportunity elsewhere. There is always hope for those who will raise their eyes from the furrows and look to the distant horizon.

MOVED ON

We're sorry there's no one to greet you
When you visit this place we've called home.
Once a covey of kids would run meet you.
Now they've grown up and all gone to roam.

The days of our lives here were trying;
The rewards for our labors were few.
But at night here there was no denying
The love that our tired hearts knew.

Today there's no hostess to treat you;
Those who lived and worked here are all gone.
We're sorry there's no one to greet you.
We all did what we could, then moved on.

- JRW, 1996

Parable of The Little Cat Who Could

She has been gone for quite a while now, but the memory of her still lingers, tender and at the same time inspiring for the spirit and tenacity she demonstrated. She came to us with the practical, if not very creative, name "Tripod."

Like most of the four-legged foster creatures in our family—in fact, all but Mittens, the first of the felines who kept us as their pets—she came to us by chance rather than by choice. Our daughter, who worked after school for a nearby veterinarian, brought her home over the Christmas holidays to help nurse her back to health. ("Just for the two weeks that the office will be closed, I promise. I just hate to think of her being there by herself in a strange place. Please?") By the end of the holiday break, we were all so attached to little Tripod that Abby's good intentions weren't tested. No longer a foundling feline, Tripod had found a home—with us.

There was a good explanation for the name, Tripod. As a result of some sort of attack on her and her kitty siblings, she was severely injured. One of her hind legs had been so badly mauled that the only way to save her was to remove it at the hip. Since she was only a few weeks old at the time, she never really knew what it was like to get around on four legs—and that was probably what made her so remarkable.

We just had to do something about that name, though. Tripod... that was OK for a male, but for a sweet little female it just wouldn't do. It had to go. Because we have had a family of ballerinas, something with a French flavor seemed appropriate. Something like Chat de Trois des Jambes (pardon my French); literally, Cat of Three Legs—or, Trois (pronounced Trwah, or Twah, if you're Southern) for short. Now, isn't that much more ladylike? But of course.

Trois was quite a sight to behold, as a kitten doing all the cute kitty things, and especially as an adult. She would go racing through the house on some imagined emergency or other, looking for all the world as if she was pushing a scooter with all her might, that solitary hind leg pumping for all it was worth. She couldn't jump very high, of course, but give her a surface she could get her claws into and Trois could climb anything. In fact, more than once she used my long pant-leg and shirt to get to the top of Mount Jack, leaving my person looking like a practice pole in the power company training yard, and my clothes turned to terrycloth.

And she could handle herself in a fight, too. If hassled by Zero or Buster—two older, bigger male cats—or by Cody the mostly English Setter foster dog of the family, she would give a loud warning hiss and roll over onto her back. Then she extended three menacing paws with sharp, long claws unsheathed, bared her teeth and waited for her unsuspecting tormentor to make the mistake of coming too close. And it was always a mistake, because Trois was *not* helpless.

No one could have convinced her that she was handicapped. In fact, Trois was the poster kitty for feline confidence and independence. And that's why I always considered her such an inspiration for mere humans. At least to those of us who took the time to notice.

She never acted as if she expected special treatment because of her unusual pedal configuration, never waited for expressions of pity or sympathy. She probably went about her life pitying those who had to drag around the extra weight of an unnecessary limb.

Anyway, whenever I see someone neutralized and immobilized by self-pity because of some real or imagined handicap—or, "challenge" if you are fond of euphemisms—I remember the example of little Trois. I feel inspired to accept the circumstances of my life, and the conditions under which I must live and work, and to say with the Apostle Paul, "I have learned the secret of contentment in every situation...I can do everything...with the help of Christ."(LB)

Parable of The Meaningful Life

It seems to come up in just about every conversation these days. Once the usual pleasantries have been dealt with, talk usually turns to whatever daily dose of doom and gloom is being dispensed by the news media. Shootings, stabbings, muggings...burglaries, car-jackings, kidnappings...fires, floods, explosions...blue-collar, white-collar and no-collar crimes...crimes against women, children, gays, blacks, aliens...crimes *by* women, children, gays, blacks, aliens... weather abnormalities, sinkholes, pot-holes...and that's just the local news. Don't get me started on State, National or World news. Or Global Warming.

It all makes me think of the bit of bumper sticker philosophy that flashed by me in traffic a few years ago. It read, "Where are we going? And, why am I in this handbasket?"

It's no wonder many have a cloud of fear, dissatisfaction and despair hanging over them. Why try to excel or succeed when there's someone awaiting the opportunity to steal what you earn, take what you have, attack you for possessing whatever they would like for themselves?

So many of our young people—although brought up in good homes, taught to obey authority, follow the rules and respect the rights and opinions of others—deduce from the news that those old values no longer apply. They see members of older generations, who supposedly lived by those standards, brought up before criminal courts, divorce courts or merely courts of public opinion, for transgressing those rules which they so loudly proclaimed to their young.

A good friend recently told me that her twenty-something son was so distressed and frustrated by the state of affairs in the world that he found it difficult to decide what to do with his life. With things in such a terrible mess all over the world, how can one expect to find and undertake some challenge that will really make a difference? Isn't that what the young and idealistic of each generation want...to do something that will make a difference in the world?

When I was growing up we had our fears and threats, too. World War II, the Korean War, the Cold War, the Viet Nam War. I grew up with talk of bomb shelters and the slogan "Duck and Cover." That was in the event of a nuclear attack. But those threats were from foreign enemies, far from our homeland.

Today, the news tells us to fear the stranger at the bus stop, on the playground, in the parking lot, and even in our schools. The car, bus, train or plane we ride may be vaporized by some fanatic's "IED" (In case you have been on the moon for the last few years, that is short for an Improvised Explosive Device.) These things are in the news every day—how can we *not* be anxious and afraid?

Dad was a wise man, the fountain of much of the wisdom that has steadied and sustained me during my life. Once, when I despaired of ever overcoming the obstacles that Life seemed to have placed in my path, he said, "Son, there's no point in worrying about things you can't control. Your only responsibility is to deal with those things you can do something about. Those are the only successes and failures you'll be judged on when you get to the Kingdom."

When Jesus sought a standard against which we should measure ourselves, He selected two simple, everyday items that all knew well: Salt and Light. He said that we should be those things to a tormented and confused world.

Salt. Crystals of salt only influence those molecules immediately adjacent to them, giving flavor and tang and delaying the effects of decay. Salt in the salt shaker isn't of any good to anyone, because it cannot affect anything that it doesn't touch. Our lives should be like salt, but we must get out of our "shakers"…come into contact with the world…thereby giving zest and helping preserve the lives around us.

Light. Not bonfires or flood lights, but the lowly household lamps that bring light to the area around them. Individual lamps revealing obstacles, making activity possible, bringing cheer where there was darkness. Even like the simple nightlight that helps calm a child's fear of the darkness.

What better life's work can we ask for ourselves than that of helping add flavor and brightening life for others?

Parable of The Mountain Man

When I was a boy I remember hearing stories about the "Old Man of the Mountain." And when you were living in Atlanta, of course, the Mountain in question was Stone Mountain, proudly proclaimed by the Chamber of Commerce as "the largest exposed granite monolith in the world." That geologically correct description doesn't do justice to the breathtaking effect on one seeing Stone Mountain for the first time. And the portion visible above ground doesn't even give a hint of the actual size of this tremendous ridge of stone extruded from deep within the earth long before recorded time.

In fact, that ridge, fed out as if by some great hand squeezing a gigantic tube of molten paste, runs for a distance of a hundred miles or more, mostly below ground, but occasionally, as in the case of Stone Mountain, reaching the surface. I remember how impressed I was in the 1970's when work on the Metropolitan Atlanta Rapid Transit System (MARTA) involved digging a tunnel below Atlanta's famous Peachtree Street, and it was revealed that they would have to chip their way through a half-mile of the granite that was part of Stone Mountain.

Anyway...as I was saying...the "Old Man of the Mountain" was often in the news in the '40's and '50's, because he was expert on how to save people who became stranded on the sides of Stone Mountain. He was born and lived most of his life near the base of the mountain, and his intimate knowledge of the peculiarities of the mountain, its surfaces and its tricky slopes, made possible the rescues of dozens of hapless and/or reckless visitors to the mountain.

When early attempts to carve a Confederate Memorial into the side of the mountain were abandoned, a simple barbed-wire fence was all that existed to keep unwary climbers from adventuring too far down the deceptive slope to view the scene below. By the time I was a teenager, that fence was pretty well beat down. Even a small child could get past it with no trouble at all, though there were plenty of signs warning of the dangers of going past that point.

Although at particular times of the day and night, especially during certain seasons, the surface itself was dangerously slippery, that wasn't the real threat. The greatest threat, after all, was psychological—the feeling that everything was all right...that one had gotten down the slope to a particular point without difficulty, and could just turn around and get back up the same way.

There was the great deception. You can reach a point where the laws of physics begin to work against you...your center of gravity is wrong, and when you go onto your toes to climb back up the incline you lose traction. That's when the feelings of panic begin to set in. Ask me how I know this, if you like.

The smart ones, getting into this situation, would stop trying to climb back up and call for help. Oftentimes that's when the Old Man of the Mountain was called to retrieve the luckless adventurer. Others were found by him after suffering a fall—several of which were fatal. One thing all the survivors had in common was that they learned a valuable lesson about testing limits imposed by others.

It is deeply ingrained in human nature—beginning in infancy—to test the fences of life...to doubt that restrictions apply to us. Just observe how hurt and surprised children are—how indignant adolescents become—when they test the rules and find justice to be swift and sure. But it's their nature to push against the limits. They find security there when the rules hold firm. And when they go beyond the barbed wire, and believe me they will, there is some comfort for loved ones in the knowledge that the Lord, like the Mountain Man, wants nothing more than the chance to bring them back to the safety and security of life within His fences.

Parable of The Tears

I think it's possible to understand a lot about people by studying what makes them cry. Of course, the era in which one lives can make a big difference in the conclusions you might reach through such a study.

For instance, when I was a boy my dad told me that big boys don't cry—only sissies did that, and I didn't want to be a sissy, did I? He told me that many times, because I had always been a world class crier. If not world class, I'll bet I could have been at least the State or Regional Champion. For me, crying was almost a track and field event...definitely not merely a vocal exercise. In my prime I was an arm-waving, running, jumping, kicking, fall-down-and-roll-around-on-the-floor crier. I originated the crying hissy fit with a triple twist. It was classic.

Although I didn't know it at the tender ages when I was perfecting the crying craft, I came by this skill naturally. My dad was quite skillful in his day, too. His crying was carefully thought out and choreographed, however, compared to my free-style technique, and was the result of some shrewd observation. He noticed that when his older sister was being spanked for some misbehavior she would stand defiantly with her arms crossed, glaring at her mother, not giving her the satisfaction of uttering even the slightest sound. The peach tree by the back porch gave out of switches, and my grandmother gave out of energy, long before my aunt showed any signs of shedding the smallest tear. But stubbornness added many strokes, however fruitless.

My dad learned from that example that the way to receive the shortest punishment was to create as much of a scene as possible. He began crying loudly even before the peach switch was pulled off the branch...his dancing, dodging and other evasive maneuvers were well in motion by the time his mother came in the door. And the volume and energy level increased until, after only two or three glancing swipes with the switch, his mother felt that she had exacted sufficient penalty and gave up trying to make contact with the elusive target. Besides, she didn't want the neighbors to believe she was committing an ax murder or other mayhem. His technique won him the commutation of many a sentenced punishment.

As I grew older, my crying became less skillful and more embarrassing to me...mostly in unseemly expression of my anger or disappointment when I couldn't have my way. In the fourth grade, when I wouldn't stay in my desk and Miss DuPree tied me to my seat with a lamp cord, I cried. When the Health Department nurse came around to give everyone in the school our tetanus booster shot, I cried. By that time, though, crying as a strategy reached the law of diminishing returns, and the punishment I avoided by crying no longer offset the reaction of my classmates—especially the girls...who by this time were becoming more interesting. That, and the fact that I started playing football with the Marietta Baby Blue Devils. And my Baby Blue Devil team mates showed no sympathy for criers.

I'm still a crier, although now the things that make me cry are quite different, and my skills aren't as artful as they used to be. I cried as I walked each of my three girls down the aisle, as I did when they were born. I'm likely to cry during a sentimental movie, but I can get by, dabbing away tears in the dark. I cry while singing with the choir at times, when I begin to think too deeply about the words of the hymns and anthems. I blubbered like a baby years ago, overwhelmed by the hopeless plight of a homeless man who didn't have the example of a Christian father like my own, who had died just a few months before that. Again recently, I cried after writing about my mother and her life and death, and how much I already missed her.

Yes, you can tell a lot about people by the things they do...and don't...cry about.

Parable of A Fellow Named Fred

My first job after graduation from Georgia Tech was as an Industrial Engineer for Deering-Milliken Textiles in Abbeville, South Carolina. Abbeville Mill was unusual in the industry because it was one of the few that started with bales of fibers at one end of the Mill and shipped rolls of finished cloth from the other. Most mills specialize, either spinning yarn, weaving cloth, or dyeing and finishing cloth after it is woven.

After I completed the initial management training program, I was assigned as a Standards Engineer in the Weave Mill. It was my job to do time studies on the various operations involved in the weaving of yarn into cloth. Those time studies were used to develop cost standards, which, in turn, were the basis for the incentive pay rates for the production workers, and, ultimately, the selling price for the finished goods.

Pretty boring, right? So, who cares about that stuff? Well, the fact is, that, since the standards set by the Engineers affects the paycheck of the mill-hands, getting accurate readings for each of the job's elements can be quite a cat-and-mouse game. Wiley mill-hands know that the standards based on their slowest pace will yield more pay later when they work at their normally faster pace. On the other hand, skilled engineers spend a lot of time learning to judge a worker's level of efficiency, and how to adjust inefficient readings to arrive at a fair standard.

That's why a high level of trust and understanding between the operator and the engineer is important if one is to come up with standards that fairly reflect the work done by the operator, without unduly increasing the cost of production. Although I was the "new kid" on the floor, I soon learned how important that trust and understanding were in gaining the cooperation of the individuals I was to study.

One of my assignments was to do time studies on a Warper. That's the machine that winds yarn onto the Warp beam, a large, spool-shaped object which is then loaded onto a loom to supply the warp for the weaving process.

The Warper Room foreman introduced me to the operator, saying, "Shorty, this is Mr. Worrill, and he's going to be working with you today. Just work normally, OK?" Then he left us to our day's work.

Shorty and I exchanged a little small talk while I was filling out my time study form, and after a minute or two I asked, "I know he called you 'Shorty', but what do you want me to call you?" He drew himself up to his full five feet four inches, stuck out his chin, and said, a little forcefully, I thought, "My name's Fred!" "Good. That's what I'll call you then. My friends call me Jack," I said. And he watched as I wrote "Fred" on the line of the form indicating the operator's name.

Maybe it was just my imagination, but I'm pretty sure that Fred relaxed after that, and I remember that we had a good work day.

Every time I saw him after that I greeted him by his name, and he seemed to walk a little taller...more like a "Fred" than a "Shorty."

I learned a lot about human nature from that experience. Fred wasn't short because they called him Shorty, but the repetition of the nickname over the years made him *feel* short, perhaps even act short. You know what I mean...feeling as if he somehow had to compensate for his size. Psychologists tell us that sometimes manifests itself in overly aggressive behavior.

The way we perceive ourselves deeply affects the way we deal with our circumstances and those around us. It is a wonderful revelation that the Lord knows us each by name...a name based upon not what we are, but who we are. And, for those who belong to Him by choice, He has a new name. We need to be like Fred, and try to spend our time living up to that new name, instead of trying to live down the name that is so often carelessly given to us by the world.

Parable of The Good and Old

On the northwestern slopes of Little Kennesaw Mountain, a short distance north of the Marietta, Georgia square, is a section called the Kennesaw Spur. It is the site of a bloody Civil War engagement, part of the battle for Kennesaw Mountain. A few hundred yards from that spot is an old farm house and several outbuildings that I have admired for many years.

Its weathered gray clapboards have kept well the secret of whether or not they have ever experienced a coat of paint. Its layout and design are plain and utilitarian, but they give it a simple charm, a quiet dignity that have appealed to me since I first saw it. The well for the house is enclosed on the covered mud porch on the north side, and the wide front porch looks out onto the two lane road that feeds traffic through Kennesaw Mountain Battlefield National Park. It's paved now, of course, but, if I remember correctly, it was still a dirt and gravel road when I first traveled it as a boy in the mid-1940's.

The closest remaining outbuilding is a small barn that is covered with the same color clapboards as the house. At the point where the boards touch the ground, there have been increasing signs of the effects a losing battle with the elements. The bottom edges have become more ragged and tattered looking, indicating the assault of wet and dry rot and testifying to the successful assault by a variety of insects. In some of the places where the boards have warped and pulled loose as if trying to escape, the original log walls can now be seen. It was never anything special, perhaps, but it had a look of strength and practical utility about it...a look that made one feel that it was exactly where it belonged.

Since we moved to a nearby subdivision, I have secretly fantasized about what it would be like to buy that old house and fix it up. I have imagined sitting in the quiet shade of that porch in a nice Brumby Jumbo Porch Rocker, calmly rocking and watching the lines of park traffic pass by. After years of such dreams, however, I've finally had to acknowledge that they are exactly that...dreams that will never be realized. Especially now.

Over the past several months, my trips past the old farmstead—I would guess it is at least a hundred years old—have revealed that years of inattention have begun to take their toll. The porch roof, sagging a little at first, has finally yielded to the irresistible urging of the goddess of gravity and fallen in. Some merciful soul recently removed it completely. The rebellious clapboards on the barn, with their warping and pulling loose from the confining nails, have been aided in their efforts to escape and have been removed. The once clean-swept yard has returned once more to a wild, natural state.

Watching this pitiful progression—or, more correctly, regression—has made me mindful of an important fact of living. Just as surely as those who planned and built that charming old farm house did so without the expectation that it would ever be found in such sad condition, they also knew that it wouldn't last forever.

When we are young, we put all our efforts into building the structures of life without a thought about the unavoidable effects of advancing age. Of course, we know that life has an identifiable beginning and a certain end, but the process of being and becoming occupies most of our time and attention. All too suddenly we find ourselves recalling youth with faulty memories.

We talk about the "good old days," knowing they were not always all that good...nor all that old, considering the span of the ages. But, like that old farmhouse, the members of each generation deserve to be recognized and appreciated for their contribution to the richness of the lives of us all—not allowed to decay and die of neglect. Let's hear it for the good and the old.

In Memory of the Good Old

As I drove past today, I was saddened
        to see the old farm house.
The porch roof, after many a decade—
        close to a century, or more, I'll bet—
        has begun to cave in.
A fine old country house like that,
        with so much character showing
        in the gray, weathered wood of its walls
        and the deep, comfortable shadows
        of that welcoming porch.
How could anyone be so careless
        as to let such an elegantly simple
        relic of the past fall into such a state?

Oh, it's been coming on for some time, now,
        noticeable first in the barn's loose boards,
        with their tattered, rotting bottoms
        slowly withdrawing from any contact
        with the disrespectful earth
        where once they had good fellowship.
Those boards were nailed over an old log out-building,
        built for function,
        certainly not for fashion.
But isn't that what character is all about?
        Function, not fashion?
        Substance, not style?

Then the plague of neglect spread to the old house, too.
The unpainted clapboards (Had they ever been painted?
        One couldn't tell.),
        the unruly shrubs, the unkempt yard.
        All signs of the forsaken.
And now, the beginning of the death rattle
        as this venerable old abode falls in on itself.

Now, I know that all that is old is not good,
Just as all that is good is not old.
But that house was once more than just shingles and wood,
And the hearts that lived there were not cold.
There were flesh and blood people, who lived,
              loved and played;
They worked hard for their clothes and for food,
And probably rocked on that porch in its shade,
Grateful for lives that were good.

Let's sing to the mem'ry of the old and the good.
Sing a song to the good and the old.
For all will arrive, though few thought that they would
When Youth was as precious as gold.
When their usefulness fails, when they've done all they could,
When on heart's hearth the ashes grow cold,
May they not be forgot, left to fall where they stood;
But honored for ages untold.

                        - JRW, 2000

Parable of The Hazardous Ones

Professor Aldrich was a fixture in the School of Industrial Management at Georgia Tech long before I arrived there, and for a considerable time following my departure. He taught a variety of courses, but the ones for which he was best known was the series of courses dealing with Business Law. That's why he was known to the IM students of that era simply as "The Judge." No one seems to know with certainty when he received his nickname, but the appellation suited him, and he seemed to like it.

With his Humpty Dumpty shape and authoritative voice...and speech that was softened somewhat by its genteel Southern Drawl... his classes were conducted with an air that approached the decorum one would expect in a real courtroom. He had a great sense of humor and a ready wit, sharpened, I suppose, by his years of verbal fencing with classes of students only slightly impressed with the finer points of Business Law.

During my years at Tech, I took three courses from Judge Aldrich. Two of them were in the area of Business Law and the third was a course in Personnel Management. They all, however, had one thing in common: They were all thoroughly salted with the same dozen or so of his favorite expressions, which were generic enough in their nature that they were equally appropriate, no matter in which class he happened to be engaged at the time.

There was one particular quotation, and its corollary, that the Judge recited in *every single class* in *each of the three courses* I took from him over a two-year period. I know this for a fact, because it was so evident in the early days of my first course with him that I kept a chart in the back of my textbook. That makes an impression after a while.

In fact, in the nearly fifty years since those classes, there has rarely been a week when I haven't had an occasion to quote Judge Aldrich on the subjects of trust and human nature and the facts of life concerning interpersonal relationships. The Judge warned repeatedly, "People are potentially hazardous." And he often followed with the observation that "Those who doubt that people are potentially hazardous are destined to learn the American way."

Cynical? Yes, of course. But that doesn't lessen the latent truth of his observations, which, by the way, are not original with him. He was just putting a modern translation to the ancient Latin legal expression "Caveat emptor/vendor"—"Let the buyer/seller beware."

Another philosopher once stated his belief that "It is better to be sometimes cheated than to fail to trust." The judge would say, "Go ahead and trust if you want to, but be aware that some 'irresponsible nitwit' will take advantage of you if he can."

Both Judge Aldrich and Black's Law Lexicon are newcomers to the idea of watching out for the potential wickedness of others, however. The Bible clearly states, "There is none righteous, no, not one." And "All have sinned and come short of the glory of God."

Anyone who believes in the innate goodness of mankind has never had, or seriously observed, small children. It is their nature to be selfish and self-absorbed, and to rail against anyone or anything that keeps them from whatever they want at any given moment. Obedience, discipline, politeness and respect for others have to be carefully and persistently taught. It is becoming increasingly clear that these lessons—if, indeed, they *are* being taught—are not being absorbed by an alarming number of today's young people.

As Christians, it is our responsibility to trust others as much as possible in our personal relationships—to be "as harmless as doves." On behalf of others, however, we must remember that "People are potentially hazardous" and deal accordingly, being "as wise as serpents."

Parable of The Heartbeat

I saw a photograph recently that brought back a flood of memories from my childhood. It was a picture of a trail through the piney woods of Callaway Gardens in Central Georgia.

The foot trail was unpaved but level, and led past a lovely group of azaleas, mountain laurel and rhododendron scattered in the open shade of the old-growth pines. Pine needles covered the ground and trail and would have muffled the sound of the creatures abiding there, as well as the tread of hikers merely passing by.

As I gazed at that appealing scene, I recalled the two summers I spent near that same area, at Bar Rest Ranch, a summer camp for boys—and a few girls, too—that was established on a western Dude Ranch theme. We lived in cabins made like bunk houses, learned a lot of cowboy skills, including some rodeo stunts which we demonstrated each Sunday afternoon for family and friends of the campers and staff.

We were awakened each morning around daybreak, had breakfast, and then the oldest of us went down to the barn, selected a bridle from the tack room and walked out into the pastures to round up and bring back the horses for the day's horse hike. We tenderfoot kids were surely a sight to watch as we tried to coax horses, already wary of our approach, to let us wrestle the bridles over their heads, and to stand still as we tried to figure out how to clamber aboard.

Even in the quiet of those mornings there was sound...sometimes an actual, audible sound, like the distant calls of those birds who had wake-up duty on that particular morning...or the thumming sound of the grasshopper vanguard leading the way as one strides through the tall pasture grass, flushing them from their hiding places. At other times the sound was something more felt than heard, like the almost imperceptible compression of the air just before the sound of an approaching car precedes it over the rise on the nearby gravel road.

On those pre-dawn walks to the barn, the quiet was so impressive that we were reluctant to talk, even at a whisper, because the slightest noise, like the skrunching of our boots on the loose gravel, seemed to fill the air around us. One could hear the dew dropping ever so softly from the leaves of the shrubs and trees, the fluttering of feathers as birds, indignant at our intrusion on their morning ritual, flew off a discrete distance to view the unwelcome spectacle of our passing.

I clearly recall the daily horse hikes into the confines of Roosevelt State Park, which enveloped most of the area around Pine Mountain. Far away from the highways and roads that connected towns, large and small, we rode quietly along trails—actually old, unpaved logging roads—carved out by bands of loggers harvesting pulpwood decades earlier. Except for the occasional clash of an iron-shod hoof on a loose stone, the only noise was from the irregular rhythm of the moseying horses, the almost-reverently murmured conversations of the youthful riders and, once in a while, the startling snuffling of one of the horses.

In the evenings, after raucous mealtimes in the chow hall, there were often gatherings around a roaring campfire with much loud talking, singing and laughing. But those rowdy moments only accentuated the silence of lights out in the bunkhouses. Once again the insistent quiet of the outdoors fell over one like a blanket, soothing, relaxing...ultimately coaxing the warm, fuzzy peace of sleep to gradually overcome the excitement of the day.

My memories of the quiet moments of those days are not frightening or oppressive, but comforting and appealing. Like the unconscious memory of Mother's heartbeat in the womb— like putting my ear to His chest and hearing the heartbeat of God. Shhhh...can you hear it?

Parable of The Pocket Full

I'm constantly surprised by the things that trigger memories—and the types of memories they generate. One night recently, we enjoyed dinner at a seafood restaurant and decided to take home the cheese biscuits that were left over. They would be the perfect complement to the home-made vegetable soup my wife was planning for dinner the next night. She wrapped them in napkins and set them in the top of her purse.

As we were turning out and locking up for the night, I asked, "Did you put the biscuits away?" With an embarrassed chuckle she said, "Oh, no! I'd completely forgotten about them. There's no telling what my purse would have been like by the time I remembered them. ..."

She may have said more, but I have to confess that I didn't hear her...my mental tape recorder was on automatic replay, and I began to see several childhood incidents projected on the screen inside my forehead. Instead of my wife's voice, I heard my mother's, asking, "What is this in your coat pocket?" and then her unrestrained giggle as she began to remove bits of the crumbled corn muffin that I had saved from the school lunch to eat later—it had been months since the last time it was cold enough for me to have worn that coat.

In the next scene I saw Mom not nearly so amused...except as she told and re-told the story years later—by then the memory had mellowed and it was easier to laugh about it. The question was the same: "What is this in your pocket?!"

It was summertime, and in the heat of the day the street was unbelievably hot, causing little glistening bulbs of tar to seep out of the asphalt paving. As the day cooled off, those shiny black teardrops were fascinating to a little boy, and I peeled off a large one to show Mom. But little boys are easily distracted, and so, while on my way to "show and tell" I took several detours. I didn't really intend to put that remarkable treasure in my pocket...but, well... And, of course, "out of sight, out of mind"—at least until the pants were washed, and half-way ironed. They were some of my favorite shorts, too.

In the final episode, I hear the same question, "What is this in your pocket?" But this time it sounds more like a Verdi duet, with Dad's voice providing the harmonizing variation, "What is that smell?" After a week in a cottage on Alabama's Gulf shore we were heading back to Atlanta in the hot, un-air-conditioned Chevrolet. There was very little parental appreciation for the lovely periwinkles—still hosting the malodorous remains of their original inhabitants—that I had saved in my bathing suit pockets to play with and enjoy when we got back home.

Pockets were meant to hold stuff...but not everything...and not forever. They were intended for temporary storage, as a convenience. What pocketbooks and "fanny packs" are to ladies, pockets are to guys...the bigger and more numerous the better. But just because we have plenty of pocket space, it doesn't follow that we have to fill and keep them full.

I am beginning to realize that it is important to distinguish those things we should hold onto and how best to hold on to them. Much of life's unhappiness and discontent stems from our efforts to gain and retain material things. We parody the Parable of the Rich Fool by ripping out our pockets and sewing in larger ones so we can say to ourselves, "Self, be cool, lie back and take it easy, 'cause your pockets are full and you've got it made, man!"

When I remember the corn muffin, the tar ball and the pocket full or periwinkles, I realize that I would have done better to enjoy them while I had them and not try to make them last longer than I should. Like the manna of Old, much of Life's treasure trove is intended to be appreciated and used, not put into our pockets for some unknown and uncertain future pleasure.

Parable of The Secure Son

I have been blessed...or, perhaps, cursed—I don't know which...with a personality trait that helps me remain calm in just about all circumstances. It drives my sweet wife crazy. It used to frustrate my dad—another so-called "type A" personality—at times, and amuse him at others. I think the best way to characterize this trait is to describe myself as having a "relaxed" attitude towards most things. I just simply don't get worried about many things that upset other folks.

It isn't uncommon for me to leave the house with only what Dad used to call rattling money—coins—in my pockets. That may foil pickpockets and the occasional mugger from making away with my riches, but it has also caused me to be embarrassed when trying to leave a parking garage or fast food drive-in, without even enough rattling money to cover the tab. I once had to leave my business card with a parking attendant while I went to the bank to cash a check to pay a 75-cent ticket. And, it's not entirely a matter of being broke, either. At least, not *that* broke. I just don't worry about whether I have money in my pocket.

My relaxed attitude (I think I'll just call it RA) manifests itself in other ways, too. Around the house, for instance. My wife, Lyn, and I agree there are a lot of things we want to do in the way of fixing up and re-doing, when we have the time and money to do them. They bother her a lot more than they do me.

Once I have determined that something can't be done immediately, I mentally file it away until the time, the money, or, maybe, the inclination, are available. I'm truthfully not trying to weasel out of them...I just don't worry about them until it's time to get them done. Lyn, however, keeps rifling through my filing system pulling these projects out and encouraging me to do something before terrible things happen (and she might cause them).

Then there are the frightening bumps in the night. She hears them and is instantly awake, tense and ready to fight or flee...or both. Yes, I heard them, too, but I am busy trying to think what makes that type of sound. If I can come up with a logical explanation, I'm ready to roll over and go back to an unworried sleep. Because I love her, I'll try to soothe her by letting her know why I believe the sound is harmless and urge her to go back to sleep, too. Also because I love her, I will get up anyway and go off to protect the castle, usually two or three beats after she has started the room to room search for miscreants.

After years of defending myself against those who are unsympathetic with my RA syndrome, inferring that I am just plain lazy, or, at best, a procrastinator, I have come to the conclusion that I simply had a very secure childhood.

I always knew that if I had a problem, or needed money—or anything else, for that matter—my Dad would be there to help me out of whatever jam I was in. The first time I had a flat tire, I went to a nearby house and called Dad. "Dad, I have a flat tire. What should

I do?" "Well, change it," he said, simple as that. So I did. After a rather expensive week-end jaunt to New York City, I once telegraphed these ten words to Dad, "Had fun in New York. Too much fun. Help. Jack" He wired me money to tide me over till I could get home. I always knew I could count on Dad. He demonstrated how the Lord wants to provide for my needs.

My RA might distress those around me, but I think one of the greatest of the Lord's blessings, aside from my salvation, is the sense of security that comes from these and countless other clear signs that there is One Who loves me and cares about whether I have those things that I really need. I can't call my Dad any longer, but I've learned that I can call "Abba! Daddy!" and be assured that He will be with me through every need...every difficulty...every trial. Amen?

Parable of The Things We Do

When I was a Freshman at Georgia Tech, my first-quarter English professor had a definite influence upon me. Professor Walker was head of the English Department, with the daunting task of teaching aspiring engineers how to communicate with normal civilians, whether through written or spoken speech. "After all," he said, "what good is it to have the most creative, elaborate solutions to the world's difficult problems, if you can't make them understood and persuade supporters to invest the money it takes to turn ideas into reality?"

In my very first paper written in his Freshman English class, I had made some high-sounding reference to "intestinal fortitude"...just as I had been taught in high school English. When the graded paper was returned to me, the Professor's note—one of those emphatic, blue pencil notes at the end of a heavy, insistent line that begins as an incisive circle encompassing the offending words and rudely jerks your eye to the margin—admonished, "If you mean 'guts,' SAY '**GUTS!**'"

I've remembered that note and quoted it many times since then. Sure, there are times when sanitary, polite speech is appropriate, probably more diplomatic; however, much of the time direct, forceful speech is superior and communicates more clearly. Too often effective communication is obfuscated (I love that word...I think it really illustrates its definition, don't you?) by awkward, stilted, words and phrases used for the sake of "political correctness."

In that same class, Dr. Walker advised, "Never get forced into writing or speaking on subjects about which you know nothing. Always approach a required topic from the standpoint of something with which you are familiar. For instance," he went on, "if you are a football player, asked to write on Keynesian economics, you might begin, 'Keynesian economics can be compared to the game of football. In football, you ...'."

A ready corollary to that advice is that one should always take the experience of one's listeners into account when crafting a message intended for them. In the words of another of my professors, "You cannot discuss color with one who is color blind."

When I was a youth, I pictured myself touching the lives of large numbers of people...perhaps as an actor, a singer, an artist, perhaps, or successful author...at the very least, an award-winning advertising copywriter. I imagined vast audiences that I would influence and impress with my creative efforts. That was and is a popular view of success.

As the Psalmist wrote, "I have been young, and now I am old ..." (Psalm 37:25) Well...maybe I'm not *old* old. There's still an eighteen-year-old lurking inside my head, but I'm well past middle-age. I have learned that those dreams and ideals are important spurs and motivations for the young; however, they can be serious handicaps for the more mature mind, dwelling on them with melancholy and bitterness for opportunities lost.

Now I take more seriously the importance of saying "GUTS," when that's what I mean. I realize that time is too short to squander it, "Commencin' to mealymouth," as Uncle Remus would say. I'm learning when to use scalpel words, and when to use chain-saw words.

Something else I'm beginning to understand is that even though I once thought it was important for me to be able to offer bits of wisdom on whatever topic popped up, nobody really expects me to be an expert on every subject...that it's all right for me to stick to those things that I know.

And when I am trying to teach to others skills I have mastered, I've learned that they will assimilate them more quickly if I can use illustrations and examples that draw from their experiences and background...to speak in language with which they can identify.

I've also learned the things we do and the things we say often nullify each other. When the things we do and the things we say are in harmony...well, I think that's successful living.

Parable of The Waiting Ones

I've already written some recollections of riding on old-fashioned streetcars, those romantic, rail-guided trams that served to transport ordinary civilians into the "big, wicked city" and home again to the serenity of their less-than-urban (but not quite suburban) neighborhoods. By the time I was ten years old or so, however, streetcars had largely been replaced by the much more modern "trackless trolley."

These trolleys were larger, and sleeker-looking, and much quieter since they ran on regular rubber tires. They still were confined by the trolley poles that drew electricity from the maze of wires overhead to give life to the nearly-silent motors that propelled them, but they were considered a great step forward into the wonderful world of modern transportation in Atlanta.

For my first three years in high school I played on the football team, and so, for several months out of the school year it would be approaching dark before we finished practice. That meant that, after the usual adolescent dawdling and horseplay with my friends, I was often at the trolley stop waiting for my bus with strings of headlights coming toward me in the lanes of traffic along Peachtree Road.

As a cool teenager...also a member of the football team...and, on top of that, an ROTC cadet, often in uniform...I thought it was definitely un-cool to stand right there beside the bus stop marker (so that the bus driver could see me and be sure to stop). I would stand back across the sidewalk and occasionally take a nonchalant glance down Peachtree to try to catch sight of the on-coming trolley.

This caused a problem...and sometimes a panic attack. There were at least three busses that came by my stop—the #24 Buckhead, the #23 Oglethorpe Express and the regular #23 Oglethorpe. I needed to catch the regular #23 Oglethorpe. But they all looked the same in the semi-dark—especially with all the headlights and traffic confusion—until they got about 50 yards away. I often asked myself, "What if I don't see the sign in time and step up to the stop so the driver knows to stop for me?" But I still didn't want to look like a jerk clinging to the bus sign.

But, you know what? No matter how many times I agonized about the bus passing me by because I didn't recognize the sign in time...I never missed a bus. I waited, watched and worried, but when the time came I always read the signs in time...always had time to step up to the stop...the driver always stopped to let me on.

I remember the story of the condemned man who was asked if he wanted to say anything before his execution, and he said, "I want you'uns to know this'll really be a lesson to me!" Well...waiting at the trolley stop was a lesson to me as a young man, and ever since. There have been countless times when I had choices to make, decisions of dire importance. I've pictured myself standing by the roadside, praying that I would be able to identify the right bus...select the correct option in keeping with the plans of the Creator for my life.

It wasn't until many years after my trolley-riding days that I came across the Bible verse that says, "And thine ear shall hear a word behind thee, saying, This is the way, walk ye in it, when ye turn to the right hand, and when ye turn to the left." (Isaiah 30:21) What an encouraging thought. And it helps me understand how I have been able to make the correct choice so much of the time. Since then I would counsel anyone struggling with difficult decisions to be encouraged by the illustration of waiting at the bus stop and the biblical promise of Divine guidance.

All of this brings to clearer focus one of my father's favorite and most-quoted verses, "Wait, I say, on the Lord." (Psalm 27:14) God bless the Waiting Ones.

Parable of The Unclouded Day

One of the great delights of my later life is the opportunity to sing in an old-fashioned southern gospel quartet. We were all members of the church choir and also active deacons when we first began to sing, so someone tagged us with the name The Singing Deacons, and it stuck. From the very beginning we have all searched for songs to add to our repertoire, sifting through many books and collections.

The other day, as I was looking through one of the many hymnals I've accumulated, I came across an old gospel standard that I thought might fit into our collection, titled "The Unclouded Day." The Refrain reads, "O the land of cloudless day! O the land of an unclouded sky! O they tell me of a land where no storm clouds rise; O they tell me of an unclouded day." As I read and thought about the words, I began to ponder the things that have clouded my skies.

I remembered how my antics as class entertainer at Park Street School resulted in Mrs. Holland, the Principal, sending me home... and Mom's promise that Dad would "have a talk with me." I recalled my fight with Edwin Edwards behind the field house at North Fulton High School. I worried about what Dad would say—not knowing he would be privately pleased that I had the gumption to stand up for myself. He said that I should come on to work after school and we could "have a talk" about it later. Not all clouds bring lightning.

There were clouds while I was at Georgia Tech...mostly, ordinary problems with classes that sometimes seemed overwhelming. On many occasions the world was put on hold while I worked through days and nights, coming right down to the deadline, to finish some crucial project or report. I don't even remember what most of them were about...or what the all-important grades were. The menacing clouds dispersed, yielding to the sunshine.

There were problems that seem silly and inconsequential now, but were real crises at the time. Like the war with the fraternity across the street, conducted with hundreds of raw eggs and bushels of rotten fruit and vegetables, and squads of commandos wielding garbage can lids as shields. Or the years when we worked for days at a time with little or no sleep in order to finish the world's most impressive Homecoming display. Some clouds are all bluster—no threat at all.

Psychologists tell us that it is the individual's *perception* of a threat—not the nature of the threat itself—that makes it a matter of concern to that individual. It is how one responds to the real clouds in life that really counts.

During my life there have been many cloudy times, some insignificant, like pulling an "all-nighter" to get a customer's job finished on time; and many others of more staggering proportion, whether or not they directly touched my personal sphere. Clouds of national and international importance, like the Kennedy assassination...the Challenger explosion, and, more recently, the Columbia disaster... a variety of police actions and wars. Or personal tragedies like the fire that destroyed my father's business...Dad's fatal heart attack...

Mom's death from a stroke. All milestone events, in a life otherwise lacking in adventure and excitement.

I've recently begun reading the reminiscences of World War II veterans belonging to my church. With little exception, they were reluctant to talk about experiences they lived through, unable to attach any importance to their contribution to our final victory. Someone once wrote that "Life is what happens while we're on our way to do something urgent."

When I reflect on the clouds of life, the real dangers, the challenges, the trials, and ask myself, "What are my resources?" I remember the voice that spoke from the cloud, "This is My beloved Son...hear ye Him." For when I listen to Him, the clouds disperse... the Son shines.

Parable of The Dumpster Diver

It hasn't been all that long ago that a new word was introduced into the lexicon of English usage: DUMPSTER. It was the name of a specific product, and was so well-crafted and promoted that it has joined the likes of jello, frigidaire, kleenex, band-aid and scotch tape as fixtures in our everyday vocabulary.

Yes, the dumpster...or the "dumper" as I heard one person call it...is definitely here to stay—although the destiny of its contents is usually just the opposite, transitory at best. Of course, it is the major fixture in any modern waste collection and handling system, and one can be found behind or near virtually every business of any size in the nation.

There seems to be no end to the things one might find put into a dumpster. There are simple discards intended to be recycled and reincarnated, finding life in new forms. Then there is ordinary garbage, trash and other rubbish headed for a dump, land-fill, or incinerator for final destruction. What a versatile and increasingly indispensable invention is the dumpster.

Recently, when we had a new roof installed on our house, the roofing contractor had a dumpster placed in our driveway to facilitate the hauling off of the debris that is part of removing shingles and old roofing. It was amazing to realize how much time and effort was saved by having that big old steel box on site.

I was interested a while back to read that a non-profit organization was having trouble with some of its collection boxes—really, just clean dumpsters. It seems that homeless people in some areas were climbing into these boxes to sleep and stay out of the weather... sometimes taking clothes and other donated items when they moved on. And sometimes the culprits were thieves who pulled up in cars and trucks, and helped themselves to the contents.

Then, there are people like my wife, who, as a department manager for a plant nursery, is regularly instructed to dispose of plants of all types and varieties when they have lost their "shelf appeal," even though they are still full of life and growth potential. To be quite fair, none in their right minds would pay good money for them. The proper business decision is to dispose of them and write them off. So...into the dumpster they go...or, at least, they're supposed to.

Several times a month she brings home a car trunk full of new "foster plants," the result of dumpster diving expeditions after one of those nursery greenhouse cleaning orders comes from on high. Perfectly good plants...just a little down on their luck, and looking a little, well, seedy (couldn't resist the pun)...which she can usually nurse back to healthy, flowering glory.

I'm not sure exactly what brought this to mind, but isn't this a lot like real life? From a practical point of view, it is often much more efficient...in terms of time and manpower, as well as resources... to just dispose of those things which have lost their shiny newness or stopped working properly. I call it the Timex Philosophy: Buy it cheap, and when it breaks or becomes blemished, just throw it away and buy a new one. We do that more and more with material things. Worse than that, though, we sometimes have the same attitude towards people.

We rapidly pass from toleration to medication, to incarceration; sometimes with a brief side step into attempts at rehabilitation. But when all else fails, into the dumpster of life they go.

One of the great revelations of my life is the realization that my Lord is a Dumpster Diver. If we become broken, He will find and fix us. Lost our shelf appeal? He'll nurse us back to a satisfying and productive life. When our original purpose is no longer possible, He'll rejuvenate and reprogram us and put us to a new use, according to His purpose and His plan. Somebody say "Amen!"

Parable of The Best Intentions

A few years ago I was having one of those afternoon visits with my mother that I cherish so much now that she is gone. We were talking about all sorts of memories, and I mentioned how Dad had always been so faithful to get her yellow roses for every special occasion. She gave a little giggle and then said, "Yes, bless his heart, he always thought they were my favorite, because I mentioned once how much my mother loved them. I never told him I really preferred pink ones. But he was always so pleased with himself for remembering those little details, that, well, I just let it be my little secret."

In forty-five years he never suspected that his good intentions missed the mark. Mom's ability to keep a secret had, itself, been a secret to those of us who knew her best. In another conversation with her, she let slip another secret, well kept from the time I was a teenager. She confessed, again with that characteristic giggle, that her favorite hymn was *not* "When They Ring Those Golden Bells." That, too, was more a favorite of her mother's than her own.

Dad wasn't the only one in the family who lost the trail while tracking good intentions. One year, when my wife was struggling, trying to teach herself to play the guitar, I got the bright idea that an Autoharp would be just the thing for her. You know, one of those zither-like things you hold on your lap and press different bars to make chords. I thought, "What an idea for an anniversary gift!" She opened the box with great excitement and told me what a wonderful and thoughtful husband I was. I was the next one to open that box, months later...and to this day she has never played it for more than a few minutes. But, hey, my intentions were good, right?

It happened again last year. My dear one, who had taken piano lessons for years as a girl, was fingering a simple tune on someone's piano and I was inspirated (you know...I had an inspiration). We haven't had a piano in the house for many years, nor do we have room for one. But, I thought, why not get her an electronic keyboard so she can brush up her skills once more? She said she really loved it, but there just doesn't seem to be a good time to play—or practice—these days. The gift did improve my GIA (Good Intentions Average), though.

A few months ago, while we were eating in our favorite Mexican restaurant, I saw the man in a neighboring booth stand up, holding his throat. His wife, fighting panic, asked loudly, "Can anybody do the Heimlich?!" I quickly got up and went to assist. I was calm and confident, my technique according to the textbook—except he was about six feet two, probably 225 pounds. I'm five ten and weigh 185. In spite of my good intentions I had to yield to another, bigger man who succeeded where I had failed to eject the offending morsel from the man's blocked windpipe. It seems that good intentions aren't always enough to get the job done.

When our good intentions fall short or go awry, our natural tendency is to try to get them back on track, to correct our error, right the wrong, so that we can proceed toward whatever goal we had in mind. However, it is clear that we cannot take it for granted that our failure can be erased and the harm, even though slight, can be undone.

There will be many times we will find that our wisdom will fail us...our intentions will far outstrip our deeds...our grandest visions will fail to inspire others...our resources will prove inadequate for our needs. When we find ourselves stymied by these realities, it is a marvelous thing to discover that—for those who love Him—the Lord bases His judgment of us on the intentions of our hearts. Whereas the world, in its limited vision and wisdom, judges an individual's motives by the results of his efforts, our all-wise God, not distracted by that outward appearance of righteousness, values only the heart's intentions. (I Samuel 16:7)

Parable of The Big Idea

My dad was a high school drop-out—actually, a pre-high school drop-out, because he quit school during the eighth grade, and high school didn't start until the ninth grade in those days. He had heard his mother and step-father talking about how the Depression and his long-term illness had put a strain on the family's finances, making it necessary for her to get a job as a retail clerk.

He decided it was time for him to do his share, so he quit school and walked into Atlanta from the community known as West End to look for a job. He found one, too, as a delivery boy for a small letter shop on Whitehall Street, just south of what is still called Five Points in the heart of downtown Atlanta. It was run by a Mr. Lecraw if I remember the story correctly. He said later he was so proud of his accomplishment that he actually spent money to ride home in grand style on the streetcar, to tell the family that everything would be all right.

As my grandmother would relate at family gatherings for decades to come, she was proud, chagrined and angry in turns when he announced his fabulous news of salvation for the family. She insisted that he tell Mr. Lecraw that he couldn't come to work for him, because he would be staying in school. But she told how Dad was just as insistent that he be allowed to do his part..."And, besides," she mimicked his pleading voice, "the man done took me!"

That's how my dad got started in the Direct Mail and Printing business five years later, with $40.00, a smile and a reputation for being dependable. Twenty-seven years later, when he wanted to put up a sign to promote his move into his own building, he hit on the slogan that would identify his business for many years...and there are many old-time Atlantans who remember it still. The sign read, "What's going up here? *I've Got An Idea!*" His reputation for creative direct mail ideas and programs brought business prospects from all over the Southeast.

During the period when I worked for Dad as an account executive (that's just a high-sounding name for a salesman), I had occasion to make a sales call on one of the large churches in downtown Atlanta. As I pulled into the parking lot, my eye was attracted to the large billboard facing Peachtree Street which read, "Come to —————— Church, Where the Folks Are Friendly!" However, a smaller sign facing the parking spaces immediately below the billboard warned, in a less than friendly tone, "These spaces for —— ——––- Church only! Violators Cars Will Be Pushed Into The Street!"

That's a slightly different approach from the Baptist church in northwest Atlanta, with a Catholic church on one side and an Episcopalian church on the other. The Baptist church had the largest parking lot, and this attracted a lot of the Brand X and Brand Y congregants to park there on Sundays, leaving Baptists without room for their chariots. That problem was solved, however, when one of the members came up with the idea of putting bumper stickers on all cars in the lot for several Sundays. The stickers read, "IT'S GREAT TO BE A BAPTIST!"

No one can deny that our ideas sometimes fail to reflect our ideals. Good ideas are hard enough to come up with, much less ideas that are consistent with our ideals. I have known many members of the "friendly" church, and you know what? They really were friendly. In fact, I was reminded recently that their pastor was one of the leaders in advancing racial unity during a period of discord and strife throughout the South. He and the pastor of the Baptist church were two of the community leaders who signed the Atlanta Manifesto which guided Atlantans away from much of the ugliness and bitterness that infected the nation at that time.

We can leave no greater legacy than big ideals followed through with big actions.

Parable of The Cheerful Giver

My dad was a generous man by almost any measure. He thought of himself as an easy mark...a soft touch...and made a show of being a hard-nosed businessman, perhaps as a defense against those who would take advantage of his good nature. When he was a young man—his "drinking days" as he called those years before he really turned his life over to the Lord—he had all kinds of friends and happy-hour companions who came to him for help getting out of one kind of mishap or another.

As a result of his availability to this parade of unfortunates and their many and varied tales of real or fabricated woe, Dad accumulated a desk drawer full of rings, watches and other items—not to mention those too large to fit in the drawer—taken as pledges securing a loan "'til payday." Most of them were eventually redeemed, but quite a few stayed in that drawer for a long time before Dad found other homes for them. I still have a very nice Elgin wrist watch that Dad gave me while I was in high school, whose former owner never came up with the resources —either emotional or material— to reclaim.

When I was a boy, there were many occasions when I would hear the telephone ring in the night. I would hear Dad answer, ask a few questions, then get dressed and leave the house, often not to return until time for breakfast. Another friend, or employee, or friend of a friend or employee, was locked up...or locked out...or had an accident...or was having family problems...and needed some help from "good ol' Fred." And Good Ol' Fred always went.

Over the years Dad accumulated a select list of "clients"... repeaters, who periodically came back to Dad like the antelopes and hyenas return to the same spring during times of drought. One of those was a young crippled man who worked for him, off and on, over a period of twenty years. Robert was a good, hard worker when sober, but he was "bad to take a drink," as they say down in the country, and was often in trouble, usually related to or resulting from his weakness. He would come to Dad every few weeks and say, "Fred, have you got...can you let me have?" Dad usually did... and he usually did.

His work with the Atlanta Municipal Court Alcoholic Rehabilitation program for several years enlarged Dad's "client base" considerably. There were Columbus and Miz Columbus, Gus and Roy, to mention a few. All were colorful characters with elaborate reasons and excuses for their sad plights. Dad accepted them without putting too much faith in their stories' veracity...or their promises to "reform and be better,"

Don't misunderstand me. Dad wasn't a gullible man. He usually knew when he was being taken advantage of. One of his most pungent aphorisms was, "I don't mind being peed on, as long as they don't think I believe it's raining." He reminded me of the motto I once saw on a friend's wall: "Blessed are those who expect nothing, for, verily, they shall not be disappointed."

Dad always had high hopes that his charitable efforts would help change the course of someone's life, but he had no false illusions about the possibilities. I asked him many times if he didn't sometimes get tired of people letting him down.

"When I get to heaven," he would say, "the Lord isn't going to ask me how I could let all those people take advantage of me that way. I don't think He will judge me based on how much or how little I helped or gave to someone. He won't even judge me by what they did with what I gave them...whether it helped them or not. I believe He'll judge me by my heart's intentions, whether I did it in His name and to His glory, and not just for my own selfish satisfaction. It's even all right if it turns out to be a wasted effort. If I did what I could, and that's the best I could do, I think He'll be pleased."

And don't be deceived into believing that the size or the value of the gift makes a difference. It needn't be much. After all, Jesus didn't say, "If you build a reservoir so thousands can drink," but, "If you give one cup of water in my name ..." Beloved cheerful givers can always be certain that they will get their reward.

Parable of First Things

I had heard about it, and I finally saw a copy of the recipe book containing the fabled formula for a locally famous country cook's rabbit stew. Following the usual listing of ingredients and proportions, the opening instruction was, "First, you get you a rabbit."

That seems at first like such an elementary instruction, doesn't it? But how often have we seen folks rushing off in all directions trying to accomplish some important task or other without first securing the most basic elements necessary for that task's successful completion?

When I was a boy, I really wanted to play the piano. Every time the family went to my grandmother's house, I wanted to pick out tunes on her piano. In those days pianos were expensive, and so were lessons, so I didn't get the chance to take up the piano until I was in high school and family finances were in better shape.

In the meantime, I talked Dad into letting me play the trumpet in the Park Street Elementary School band. A trumpet was much less expensive, and the school band director gave me the only lessons I had...free, of course. I learned to play "Twinkle, Twinkle, Little Star" and "Hear Dem Bells," and perhaps a few other songs that the band practiced in the allotted one day a week. There was one problem, however. I never learned to finger the sharps and flats, so I would just not play whenever they were indicated in the music. And, when you are the only trumpet in an eight piece school band, it's pretty obvious when you fail to play notes here and there. I gave up the trumpet after the seventh grade.

I had the chance to take piano lessons when I was a Junior in high school, but by that time I was easily frustrated, because I knew how the music was supposed to sound and couldn't make it sound that way. I gave up the piano after the eleventh grade.

I realize now what the trouble was with my trumpet and piano careers: I wanted to *be* a trumpet player and a pianist, but I was unwilling to *become* a trumpet player or pianist. I wanted the results without first "getting the rabbit"...I lacked the discipline to do the first things and develop the technical skills that would be necessary to successfully play the trumpet and piano.

I'm not the only one with that problem, either. I am constantly amazed to discover people who are technically and intellectually superior to us normal civilians, who want to establish laws and theories and to espouse principles without first getting the rabbit... accepting the foundation of our most basic existence.

All sciences are based upon the reliability of rules of order. Scientific laws are founded upon the ability to observe recurring phenomena and duplicate the results. All too often, however, scientists, philosophers and other self-proclaimed thinkers propound their laws and theories without coming to grips with the origin of those rules of order, the power behind those recurring phenomena.

It isn't enough to recognize that there are creatures and objects in the world, and to construct laws based upon their existence.

Theoreticians insist that if you shake a sack containing all the parts for a watch an infinite number of times, you could, theoretically, assemble a working watch. But they miss the point—they haven't got the rabbit. Where did the parts come from in the first place? The existence of a watch should be ample proof, to the seeker for truth, of the existence of a watchmaker...every cake is evidence of a baker.

A creation must, by definition, have a creator. All recurring phenomena must have a power source to originate, to organize and to sustain them, keep them going. That power...that Creator...we call God. "Seek ye first...God and His righteousness." (Matthew 6:33)

Parable of A Certain Sound

I've always been in awe of good poets. I admire the ability to construct well-crafted rhymes, to harmonize artistically structured ideas and send readers' imaginations exploring. Whether the writer's musings are profound, meticulously worked out in complex rhythms of word and thought, or ingenuous inspirations clearly and succinctly expressed in crisp verse, my initial reaction is likely to be, "I wish I'd said that!"

After a few years of writing advertising copy, I tried my hand at some creative writing. My first experiment was a series of free verse poems inspired by a group of photos I had taken. Whether they were any good or not I'll never know. I presented the only copies I had to a college English professor I knew and asked for his advice and critique—he promptly lost them among the stacks of student papers he handled, and they have not seen the light of day since.

My next effort at free verse was for an anniversary gift for my wife. "Our Journey Together" compared our marriage to the passage of the full moon across the mountain-bordered night sky as depicted in a photograph taken in the Smokey Mountains National Park.

On the road from Gatlinburg to Cades Cove in the Park there are several scenic overlooks which afford a magnificent panorama of the mountains as you make the first ascent from the Visitors' Center. Lovely and satisfying as it was for the morning trek to Cades Cove, the vista was absolutely breathtaking as we descended after a day in the Cove's idyllic peace.

We paused at one of those overlooks to absorb the scene as the clouds cycled from light pink to fiery orange to deep purple to the dark, mottled gray of night. The full moon seemed unnaturally large, and though it appeared to grow more radiant as we watched, it couldn't be seen to move at all. However, when our eyes turned to other sights, it seemed that, once released from our gaze, the moon resumed its journey across the night sky, hastening to keep its tryst with the western horizon. Its position had clearly changed when we focused upon it again.

In "Our Journey Together" I intended to say that our marriage was similar to that scene. It may seem ordinary and unremarkable in its everyday episodes, but when viewed at a distance, through the filters of time and experience, its uniqueness and accomplishments are evident.

The first few people who read this new work told me they just didn't get it. My tender, writer's feelings (or "feelers" as my sister used to say) were sorely bruised. When one's ideas and emotions are exposed to the opinions of others, there is a definite sense of vulnerability that leaves one feeling like the proverbial "deer in the headlights"...and it's quite unsettling.

An English professor once told our class that good poetry never needed to be explained, that it should be able to speak for itself. After all, he said, poems are subjective and affect people in various ways, so don't fret over those who fail to understand profound thoughts.

(Following that pronouncement, he explained and analyzed the poem assigned for that class.)

I find that a lot of life is like that. We spend a lot of our time going about, doing what we think of as good, worthwhile things; at the day's end, we look in the mirror and, like Little Jack Horner, say, "Oh, what a good boy am I!" But those "good boy's" don't satisfy the creative mind unless others also recognize our accomplishments with proper respect and appreciation.

Scripture asks, in I Corinthians 14:8, if the trumpet gives an uncertain sound, how will the people know how to respond? If one's sentiments and observations are worthy of other's response—if they are to speak to their hearts—they need to be clearly expressed. I believe God-given talents are intended to be used in a way that enlightens and benefits others. I'm still not sure my work since those early efforts gives forth a "certain sound," but I'll keep working on it.

OUR JOURNEY TOGETHER

The quiet course of the full-blown moon
Across the infinite, splendor-studded
Black velvet of night
Appears, to the wondering eye,
To promise the Traveler
An eternity of discovering,
One by one,
The endless delights of the Lord's creation.

But, from gaze to gaze,
That unperceived pace
Is seen to speed the Traveler
From glory to glory
As if in an instant.
And it is gone.

Just so, our love,
Full-blown from its rising,
Seems at each moment
To be set like a jewel
In the crown of God's Time
For all the glorious aeons.

Yet the produce of our love
Awakens our hearts once and again
To the sweet sadness of fleeting years.
Sweet, because of the tenderness,
    The warmth,
        The boundless joy
Of each moment remembered.
Sad, because our poor minds
    Can scarce recall
        Or relive
The countless delightful details
Of our journey together.
    - JRW—1970

Parable of A Name That Is Known

"My name is Worrill, and that sounds like 'squirrel'." That's the way my Dad introduced himself to new acquaintances as a young man, and he continued that practice throughout his life, as he addressed many types of groups—not a few times as a lay preacher speaking to church groups of all sizes. He must have begun that practice at a young age, because it was possible to identify friends from his youth by the "Squirrel" nickname they occasionally applied to him.

Another way to recognize Dad's family and friends from "the old days" was that they always called him "Jack." Apparently there was already a close family member named Fred when he was a child, so someone took to calling Dad Jack in order to avoid confusion. When that early relative made an untimely departure, and Dad was free to resume the name Fred, "Jack" was tossed back into the hat, resting unused until I came on the scene.

Anyway...I was named Jack in honor of Dad's boyhood nickname, and Reynolds in honor of his step-father, Ned Reynolds, a kind, old-style Southern gentleman. Since Mr. Reynolds was not the birth parent (as the politically correct would say today) to my father and his siblings, he insisted that they call him "Partner," which was softened in the typical Southern way to "Podnuh." That's what all the adults called him...we kids called him "Pa-Pa."

When it came to nicknames I was pretty lucky, I guess. The only ones I have had (at least, as far as I know) were fairly innocuous.

In high school I was "Happy Jack" (I smiled a lot, and cracked a lot of jokes) or "Whirly Bird" (because my last name sounded like a popular TV show of that day). My favorite name is the one I bear as a grandfather. All the grandkids—and our daughters and their husbands—call me "FooFoo." I'll tell you about that some other time.

Have you ever noticed how much bearing names have on our lives? There are times when the meanest thing kids can think of to do to each other—after hitting and biting are forbidden—is to call names. The earliest ones aren't too bad. Being called "Doo-doo head" probably never traumatized anyone, but how about "Fatso," "Elephant Nose," "Pizza Face" or "Beaver Teeth?" Some of those names can cause life-long psychological problems.

It is a great blessing to have a name to live up to, rather than one to live down. And, regardless of the lesson in the song about a Boy Named Sue, that's why you'll probably never meet a Judas Iscariot Jones...or a Benedict Arnold Brown...or even a Simple Simon Smith.

Sometimes we assume names that are fanciful or deceiving, like the so-called "handles" used on CB radios, or the pseudonyms adopted when we write Dear Abby or enter on-line chat rooms. Like the Mighty Wizard of Oz, we try to keep others from looking behind the curtain...we adopt user names to identify us while simultaneously concealing who we really are.

A historical standard for names was that they revealed either details about one's character or personality or, perhaps, the parents' hopes and aspirations for them. It is natural to make the connection of an individual with his family name. In the South, a common question upon making a new acquaintance is, "Who are your people?" Who is behind the name you bear?

A reality that threatens some and encourages others, is that God knows each of us by name. There is a great Gospel chorus that goes, "He knew me, Yet He loved me." Not only has He identified us and loves us anyway, but He has given each believer a new name, untarnished and unsullied, bearing no remnant of the shame, sin and disgrace associated with our earthly life.

As another gospel song puts it, for all who have put their trust in Him, "There's a New Name Written Down in Glory." That name identifies us as God sees us...as He intended us to be...consistent with His Will for us. Truly a name to be lived up to. Praise His Name!

Parable of The Open Hand

Have you ever stopped to think how complex we humans are psychologically? What we desire and drive for in one moment we dread and dodge in the next. We are jealous and fiercely protective of our liberty and privacy, and at the same time we indignantly insist upon safety, security and protection...insurance from all hazards.

You only have to observe a toddler for evidence of this paradox. As their diminutive personalities develop, they pull free of the parents' hands and crawl, walk and eventually run in the opposite direction. Then when they meet an obstacle, or a stranger, or some furry creature curious to have just a small taste of them, they are eager...in a panic, even...to be picked up and held and delivered from harm.

I clearly remember my loving Mom, with her hand firmly grasping the seat of my first "big boy" bicycle as I anxiously tried to pedal and stay upright at the same time. "Don't let go!" I screamed over my left shoulder as I felt the bike begin to waver. "I've got you," she said. Then, "Keep pedaling, you're doing fine." "Don't let go!" "You're OK!" came the loving reply, suddenly sounding more distant. I searched over my left shoulder, seeking that reassuring presence, but she was standing back at our driveway, cheering me on. SHE HAD LET GO!

"I SAID 'DON'T LET GO!'" I wailed as I ran up on the curb two doors down the street and sprawled in the grass, crying and feeling betrayed. It wouldn't matter until a little while later that I had gotten that far, riding my first bicycle all by myself. If she hadn't opened her hand and let me go there's no telling how long I would have stayed grounded in the driveway of the white brick house at 50 Willowwood Circle.

My first swimming lesson wasn't much different...my Dad's hands buoying me up as I got the hang of kicking my feet and stroking with my arms. The first time he removed his hands I sank like a bullion-laden Spanish galleon in a typhoon, only to shoot to the surface spewing and crying and fuming. "You let me go!" I protested, "And I wasn't ready!" "But you're all right, I see," came the calm reply. "Yes, sir...but I wasn't ready."

Then the tables began to turn. I learned to drive, and decided it was time for Mom and Dad to let me go. In view of these changing circumstances, they became reluctant to do so. As an adolescent I couldn't understand the change in attitude—I resented it. Later, as a parent, and now as a grandparent, I understand it all too well. Not only is it frightening the first time we are let go...it is a sobering experience for the one standing back with open hands, having let go.

There are times, whether we be very young or very old, when we desire the assurance of the firm Hand grasping us, guarding us, guiding us. Even when the appointed time arrives, and the Hand opens to grant us the liberty and freedom we so desperately sought, we yearn, in our more insightful moments, for the sensation of the Hand supporting, soothing and steadying us.

Whether one is painfully dependent or purposefully independent, one must keep in mind the image of the Open Hand. It is no accident of prose that the Bible makes so many references to the Hand of God. One of my favorite verses is Psalm 95:7. "...we are the people of His pasture and the sheep of His hand." People are in the pasture to work, and that's our job; sheep of His hand are favored pets, loved and cared for, and that's our pay, tendered by His open Hand.

Another favorite "hand" verse is Psalm 3:3, "But thou, O Lord, art...the lifter up of my head." I remember times when I was hurt or sad and felt my mother's open hand gently placed under my chin, raising my head to look into her loving eyes as she spoke words of comfort and cheer. A grasping hand can never clutch as much as one that embraces all with open fingers.

Parable of The Power Of The Petty

I worked for hours over a period of several days recently on a computer program that transcribes music from my old vinyl LP albums onto compact discs. The program is a simple, "For Dummies" version of the type of program that professional sound technicians use to make high-quality commercial recordings, but it allows me to make pleasing CD's for my own use.

The result of using this program is that I can once more enjoy the music I listened to as a young person...music that saw me through many hours of college study...music that Lyn and I courted to...music that our children heard as they grew up. You know, back when music was something you could listen to with melodies you could sing, or harmonies and arrangements that could serve as a calming background for activities—even something you could go to sleep to.

Since I installed the program I have transcribed several dozen LPs, each one taking up to two hours to get "just right." (Anyone who spends much time working with computers knows this to be true...the time saved by the computer in processing is a trap for many of us who spend a tremendous amount of time doing things we wouldn't bother with otherwise.) Anyway...as I mentioned earlier, I had invested a good bit of time on a project I had recorded off the local PBS FM station, when it happened.

After cleaning and adjusting the sound quality of the program, I tried to combine two separate segments into the final mix...and, without warning, suddenly one of them disappeared. Worse, the surviving segment duplicated itself where the missing one had been. Worst of all, in every place I searched for the missing segment, the surviving file cloned itself, replacing what had originally been there. Don't you just hate it when that happens?

Boy! was I irritated...and my irritation was aggravated...and it was fortunate that Buster Kitten was in his final resting place in the Peaceful Pet Garden, because it was definitely "kick the cat time," if you know what I mean. I felt like I just needed to smack somebody. (Not that I ever would have, of course, but I certainly felt like it.) It really cast a pall on the weekend, and I moped around for several days.

Psychologists have noted that one of the most common responses to frustration is regression, where one reverts to progressively more childish behavior. Well, that was me, all right. Regression with a capital R-E-G-R-E-S-S-I-O-N.

However, one advantage of age is that those first reactions don't stay with me as long as they once did. Even while my stomach was still in a tangle of disappointment, my spirit (more accurately, the Holy Spirit) began to take charge. The upsetting of my plans didn't register on even the most delicate instruments measuring the Richter Scale. The tides flowed, the stock market was unmoved, the Earth and its fellows coursed onward in their orbits, and, in the final—and honest—analysis, all was right with the WORRILL...in spite of this petty set-back.

I've come to recognize this truth in other aspects of my life as well. There are so many petty things and minor events that can spoil my day and rob me of my joy if I let them. As I've written before, "It's not the lions and tigers that get us, it's the gnats."

I understand that the adversary has no power over the major things in a believer's life. He can't have my soul or keep me out of the Kingdom. The best he can do is to poke his evil, bony finger into my mind and try to distract me with petty things, make me miserable, angry or afraid.

When petty things threaten to overpower me, I remember what my Mom used to tell me. "You just tell him, 'I'm saved by the blood of Jesus, and I command you in His name to leave me alone and go to...where you belong!'" And you know, that really works. I commend it to you.

Parable of The Questioned Answer

An important thing I've learned about the Lord's provision in answer to my prayers is that the delays in His answers most often seem to allow time for the so-called "urgent" needs to be resolved—or to resolve themselves—usually making any obvious divine intervention unnecessary. God's waiting room is, to me, a lot like a railway sidetrack—where the "local" waits, while a few yards away the "express" roars past. Then, its patience rewarded, it re-enters the main line to resume its purposeful journey.

So often my urgent and anxious petitions must seem to the Loving Almighty like the whiny "Are we there yet?" of a favored child, to be answered by the patient reply which tells all we need to know: "No, but it won't be long now."

Some circumstances call for an immediate and obvious answer to prayer. We're inclined to call those experiences miraculous. But I think that—better than a miracle, which is a happening which goes against nature—it is the normal response of an attentive Guardian, like my daughter catching her baby before it falls out of its chair or knocks over some precious object.

However, more often, the Lord hears our prayers and, patiently and in perfect order, goes about directing ordinary events to bring about an answer that is consistent with His will and nature—an answer, by the way, which may or may not match our specific request, but which perfectly meets our real need. I have a clear life example of this kind of answered prayer.

I was introduced to the principle of praying specific prayers by my sister and her new husband, a member of the staff of Campus Crusade for Christ. David said that God is not offended by our sincere prayers which attach specific details to our prayer requests, but rather is pleased to be able to reward acts demonstrating such faith in His providence.

About that time my dear Lyn decided she wanted to have one more baby...specifically, she was willing to try for a boy. We already had two beautiful girls, and were delighted with what the Lord had provided, but we would like a boy this time, if it pleased the Lord.

So, as the high priest of the family, I prayed this specific prayer, "Lord, you are Creator of the chemistry, biology and physiology of reproduction, and you know exactly the conditions and timing that will have to be in effect in order for us to have a boy. We pray that you will keep us from being able to conceive until everything is right for us to have a boy. Thank you for your answer to this specific prayer."

We tried, without results, for almost a full year before Lyn was "found to be with child." Bingo! Since the Lord had obviously heard and answered our prayers, we proceeded with all the preparations for our boy...clothes, name, toys...everything fell into place. My dad even tried to bribe us to name his expected grandson after him, but Lyn's mind was set on a "Junior."

The day of labor arrived and the anticipation was great. Then, after a long day in the fathers' waiting room, came the physician's announcement over the intercom, "Mr. Worrill, you have a beautiful, healthy baby...girl." To which I silently prayed the specific prayer, "Uhmmm ...Lord, did you by any chance get the orders mixed up somehow?" But He clearly hadn't.

So...our boy's name is Abigail. But I'll tell you this: If I had made a list of those things that I expected a son to mean to a father, Abby filled the bill to a tee. After her sisters began to pursue young-womanly things, she remained as my companion, my buddy, my expedition mate.

Yes, the Lord answered our specific prayer in His way. I prayed for a boy by gender. He gave us a "boy by temperament." He knew He created me as a daddy of daughters. I'm satisfied and happy that—as one father said—all my boys were girls, and I got all my sons ready-made.

Parable of The Risk Taker

I listened as several NASCAR fans discussed the appeal of stock car racing. There is the thrill of the sight of dozens of automobiles, painted in a blinding array of colors, hurtling around an oval racetrack at a frightening pace. And the mind-numbing roar as those powerful engines fling tons of rubber, steel and plastic into banked turns and hurl them along crowded straightaways. Not to mention the throbbing excitement of the cheering, screaming crowds of race fans filling the grandstands and flooding the infield area.

Yes, of course there is all that. But what draws many fans back, those sound bites that make the 11 o'clock news, are the crashes. It could be the little bumping between two chariots competing for that choice place in the pack of vehicles, or the encounter with the retaining wall that proves once again that two particles of matter can't occupy the same place at the same time. Better yet, the flaming show stopper that tumbles cars in all directions, sending sheet metal and plastic parts flying away and fireballs with clouds of black smoke billowing skyward. Now THAT'S SOMETHING! That's what compels many to stay glued to the TV set for hours at a time. I confess that the wrecks are the only thing that I don't find boring. But that's just me.

With that in mind, I listen with fascination to those who have been enticed to watch with almost hypnotic intensity the current TV fad called American Idol. Most of those who watch the show even casually are especially drawn to the first half-dozen shows in each series, where the initial auditions are held in various cities across the nation. I'm convinced that they watch those auditions with special interest because that's where most of the spectacular entertainment car wrecks happen. That's where egos are battered and crumpled, and hopes go up in flames.

For the benefit of the occasional aborigine wandering in the Outback, who may not know, the American Idol show is one with a hopeful handful of talented young people—and a multitude of others with little or no talent as performers—who expose themselves to the merciless, brutal truth of a team of judges led by an unsympathetic Simon Cowell and an audience of millions. And, let's face it: Many of these early contestants *are* truly awful.

I have to confess that I don't have the stomach to watch this portion of the show. Why would anyone subject themselves to this ultimate opportunity for rejection and humiliation? I find watching and listening so painful that I can't take more than a few minutes of it at a time.

A friend of mine recently asked a teenager who watches the show regularly and with great interest, "Who in his right mind would do such a stupid thing and bring on so much pain?" The young person answered, "I enjoy the show. I admire them…even the bad ones—at least they're taking a shot at it." And, you know what? I think that youngster was on to something.

There's an old saying that "You can't tell 'til you try." On the other hand, there's the parody on an old inspirational poem that goes,

"So I tackled the thing that 'couldn't be done'…and I couldn't do it either." And I suppose that is the reason why most of us hold back from challenges—the fear that we will fail. The fear that it could be *us* in that car wreck.

A famous athlete once said, "You'll miss the goal with 100% of the shots you don't take." Another wise man wrote "I'd rather be a has-been than a never-was any day." Go out there and head for the goal; you just might make it. Besides, it's always harder to hit a moving target.

The Bible has a good many bits of advice for risk takers. One of my favorites is Joshua 1:9; "Have not I commanded Thee? Be strong, and of good courage, for the Lord thy God is with thee whithersoever thou goest." With every risk there is a potential car wreck…but you can't pass the Finish line if you never leave the Starting line. So go ahead…take a shot at it.

Parable of **The Sanctified Ones**

Have you ever been in one of those homes where the sofa and chairs had those clear plastic covers over them? I remember when they first became popular, and my grandmother had them on the living room furniture for a while. They were uncomfortable, hot and they stuck to you in that era when "air conditioning" meant open windows and an oscillating electric fan.

They did the job, though, when there were a lot of grandkids around, and when you did what you could to keep the "good" furniture looking nice for *real* company. In plenty of families the Living Room was off limits...at least to everyone but parents and visitors. Nice things were costly and were saved mostly for show—certainly not for everyday use.

When our children were young, we decided that it was more important to enjoy what we had, including the kids, so the Living Room Rules were relaxed quite a bit. In addition, we always had a Den where we could all lounge around a little more freely, so we didn't worry quite as much about keeping the "good furniture" in protective custody.

However, our dinnerware was a slightly different matter.

Our two families were quite active in our church for years before we married. As a result, our wedding invitations brought us an embarrassment of riches in the way of many very fine wedding gifts. Silver flatware, beautiful sets of china, lovely crystal...those things were more conventional as wedding gifts then, and, unlike today, although very fine gifts, they didn't require the giver to take out a second mortgage on his home.

In short, we were blessed with a startling amount of "good" silver, china and crystal. It has always been kept safely put up and out of the way, waiting for just the right occasion. And, to this day, our daughters know what it means when Lyn offers to get out the good silver, china and crystal—it means someone special is coming to dinner.

And we're not unusual in this. I'm sure every family has its own lot of things packed away and out of sight, set aside for use when one of those extraordinary events occurs. It could be as simple as the good placemats, the good sheets and pillowcases...you know what I mean.

You might be interested to learn that this is Biblical. That's right, Biblical. The Holy Spirit led some writers of the New Testament to use the Greek word *hagiazo*—to make holy, clean, pure, chaste; purify; consecrate, set aside—which is translated "sanctify, sanctified," and is the word used to refer to one of the significant results of the salvation of the believer.

In many places, we are admonished to *be* holy, because God is holy...to *be* perfect (in the sense of always being in the process of becoming perfect), even as God is perfect. When we are honest with ourselves, however, we must admit how impossible that is for us in our natural state. At that point, if we ask Jesus to take charge of our lives, the Holy Spirit makes us holy, cleans and purifies us, and sets us aside for His special purpose. We become His *good* furniture, His *good* silver or china...no longer to be counted among the everyday things—but sanctified.

Unlike you and me, however, God doesn't sanctify items for show. He doesn't close off the place where He keeps us to be used as museum pieces. When He sanctifies us...cleans us up and makes us holy...He has a useful purpose in His Mind.

The Lord's wood shop contains the finest tools, in good condition...but you can bet that there'll be sawdust and wood shavings on the floor. We are sanctified, set aside, for work; and the only way we believers will be judged when we reach the Kingdom will be on the basis of whether or not we faithfully went about the work for which we were specially intended. The sanctified furniture, the sanctified silver, the sanctified soul will all show the patina of use.

Parable of The Shared Light

It was time for the Children's Message, and the children had come streaming down all the aisles as usual to collect on the steps leading up to the Pulpit platform. On this occasion, however, the one prepared to present the message was Miss Shirley, the Minister to Children, instead of the pastor.

After a few introductory remarks, she asked the children what she and Scott, the Youth Minister were holding. They each held a candle. Shirley's was unlit, while Scott's was burning brightly. She asked Scott to give her his flame, and in response he held his candle to hers until it, too, flamed vigorously.

Shirley asked, "Did you see what happened just then? I asked Scott to give me his flame, and he did. But then what happened to his candle? Did it go out because he shared his flame with me? Of course, not. His flame actually doubled in size as a result of sharing it with me, didn't it?" She went on the say that that is the way sharing works. Shirley then applied that principle to sharing our Christian relationship with others.

As she proceeded to tie that idea to the upcoming spiritual emphasis in our church program, my mind was focused on a personal experience with my three girls as they were growing up. This candle demonstration was the perfect illustration of a teaching I had tried to communicate for years.

I attempted for many years to explain how much I loved each of my dear girls. I have told each of them many times that she had "all my love," and that "love is the only one of God's gifts that we can give all of to someone and still have all of it left over to give to someone else."

If only I had been wise enough to have thought of the sharing of candlelight as an example of that kind of love. I see now that it is so perfect. The burning wick brought heat and light and life to the cold, dark and lifeless wick—doubling its reach without losing any of its own brilliance—and could do the same for many others just like it, multiplying its effectiveness countless times. And until the original flame is extinguished...or when the candle is consumed...it remains undiminished by the sharing.

Well, love is like that, isn't it?

Parable of **The Undetected Input**

At a recent event to highlight the many ministries of our church, I happened by the booth for the Music Ministry while the Minister of Music was setting up the Audio Visual projector. The Power Point program which uses the computer to coordinate the sound, slide show and special visual effects was not cooperating.

As Paul conjured over the keyboard expectantly, the screen flickered a time or two, then gave the unresponsive response, "No Input Detected!" It didn't take him long to correct the situation and get the presentation under way, but I had already received my "message du jour."

My first impression as I read that cryptic message—NO INPUT DETECTED—was, "Boy, have I been there!" I couldn't count the many times in my life when I have sought advice, guidance or inspiration, and could find no one who was ready or able to help me out.

There is a phrase from a song my dad used to sing out, loudly enough for us all to hear, when we failed to respond to his summons. He would serenade us with, "I called and I called, but nobody answered ..." (After years of searching, I found "Nobody Answered Me" on Google.)

Not only is it a fact when working with computers, but it's also true when dealing with people, striving with circumstances and seeking the Lord's guidance in dealing with decisions: There are times when there's no input detected from the other side...when, no matter how urgently I call, I can't detect an answer. What are we supposed to do when that happens?

There are two particular blessing/curses of modern communications—well...of course, there are more than two, but two that I find especially irksome. The first is Call Waiting, and the second, which is made more aggravating by the first, is the Flash or Hold button. I know, one can argue there are times when it is good to know an expected call is coming through while you're in the middle of another conversation. However, am I the only one that thinks it rude to be in mid-sentence and hear, "Oh, I have another call coming in, can you hold? (Click.)"

I don't have to be on Hold for long before I begin to understand that the Other Caller is more important that I am. And the longer I have to hold, the more I resent it.

(While I am on pet communications peeves, I might as well put in my vote against those automated answering systems. "The party you are calling is much too busy to talk to someone like you. If you're willing to wait thirty minutes or more press "1," If you have nothing better to do and want to listen to some dreadful wallpaper music press "2," If you're a big-shot and think your time is too important to spend waiting for us to pick up the phone, please press "3" to leave a message, or hang up gently and go away. Thank you, and have a nice day.")

One thing that I have learned, however, is that, though people may ignore us, and modern communication systems may mock us, it can never be said that when we approach God with a problem, a question or a request He fails to give us an answer. "But," you might protest, "what about all the times that I prayed and ..." I've had the same thought myself...many times, in fact.

However, I haven't been troubled by that thought since someone pointed out that God answers our prayers in one of three ways: "Yes," "No," and "Not Now." (All right, it's true that almost all parents use "Not now" as a sneaky substitute for "No"...but not our God.)

The next time your Prayer Monitor reads "No Input Detected," remember what Oswald Chambers said, "God answers prayer in the best way—every time. However, the evidence of the answer in the area we want it may not always immediately follow."

Chambers also said that Jesus never mentioned unanswered prayer, because He knew that God *always* answers. And that's input you can count on.

Parable of Trombones and Tomatoes

I lived at home while attending college. I didn't own an automobile at the time, and depended upon my dad's schedule for transportation to and from school. The result was an unusual amount of time spent in the Georgia Tech library while waiting for my ride—studying, talking with classmates, napping and, often, simply killing time.

One day, while I was conspiring to assassinate an hour or so, I happened upon a little book of verse by James Weldon Johnson, titled "God's Trombones—Seven Negro Sermons in Verse." Johnson wrote that the title was suggested by the voice of a memorable preacher he had heard, "a voice—what shall I say?—not of an organ or a trumpet, but rather of a trombone, the instrument possessing above all others the power to express the wide and varied range of emotions encompassed by the human voice—and with greater amplitude."

Johnson's sermons became some of my favorite verse, eloquently written and arranged in a format that almost allows one to experience the sound and forcefulness of a live service. One can all but see the earnest perspiration on the brow, hear the pulpit resound with the drumbeat of a fist pounding in emphasis of key words and phrases.

As I have thought over the years about these "trombone concerts from the pulpit"—and I have heard some, delivered by devout believers from many backgrounds—I have gained an unexpected insight into the nature of Christian ministry and service. It is an insight based upon the idea of each believer serving the Lord with the attitude of being God's Trombone.

After all, what is it that makes a trombone solo memorable? It isn't the vision of the shiny, highly polished brass tubing as it catches and reflects the spotlight. Or the graceful curled shape, or the silent action of the slide as it traverses from note to note in seamless transition.

If you attended a trombone recital, I doubt you would come away uttering such praises as, "Wasn't that a lovely trombone?" or "Did you notice how smooth the action of the slide was?" No, I suspect that any compliments and praise would be directed to the musician who used the trombone to produce the music which uplifted and inspired the audience.

The trombone has only one job: to remain open so the musician can direct the flow of air through it to produce melodic sound...to be available, responsive to the touch and breath of the musician. A trombone doesn't have to do anything...indeed, is incapable of producing effort...in order to make music. It is its nature, yielded to the hand of the musician, to make music.

I once told a Sunday School class that you could not expect to go into your garden, put your ear close to a tomato plant and hear the sound of it straining to squeeze tomatoes out of its stem-tips. It is the nature of the tomato plant, when properly tended, watered and fed, to produce tomatoes, without thought, planning, strategy or expenditure of earnest effort. It is as ludicrous to think a tomato plant could produce larger tomatoes by trying harder as it is to think of a trombone making more melodious tones by dint of additional effort.

What is true of trombones and tomato plants is just as true of Believers. Oftentimes we go about doing "good stuff" thinking we are serving the Lord, when we are really like rebellious trombones, pulling our slides from the hand of the Musician, trying to make holy music in our own way. That's when all our best efforts "turn to prunes," as one of my friends used to say.

When the Spirit dwells within us, it is our nature to do the good works for which the Musician designed us. Not all of us are trombones...some are tomato plants...but if we will only remain open to our nature, others will be blessed through us. Has anyone praised the Musician, the Master Gardener, because of what they have heard or tasted through you lately?

Parable of The Insistent Input

You could hear them coming long before you could see them... even before you could identify where they were coming from and where they were headed. It wasn't an unfamiliar sound, especially at this time of year, but I was out on my regular morning walk around the neighborhood, so I was able to pay more attention to it than usual.

There's an 18-acre lake in our sub-division, so the sound of Canada geese arriving and departing is a common occurrence—in the Spring and Fall their V-formations are like large, noisy cursors moving across the suburban skies, pointing the way toward their seasonal feeding places. This morning, though, there wasn't the usual avian "call and repeat" chorus with the leader sounding a call which was echoed by the following members of the flock.

No, on this occasion there seemed to be only one voice...an insistent, intermittent honking that apparently had been going on for some time before its owner came into earshot, because my first awareness of it was as if I was joining a broadcast in progress with the volume gradually being increased as they approached. And it continued, unabated, until the splash-down in the lake a few seconds after they passed overhead.

The thing about this particular experience that made me laugh out loud was to see that the goose doing the honking was one of a pair—geese mate for life, you know—and was not the one flying in front. So the picture was of two geese, the leader flying silently—to my mind's eye, stoically...with concentrated determination—and the mate, bringing up the rear with insistent and incessant honking, as if engaged in an extended harangue.

In all fairness, it was impossible to tell whether the leader of this seemingly ill-matched duo was male or female. And, since I do not speak goose, I couldn't tell whether the air-borne tirade was an extreme case of "back wing driving"...some sort of feathered rant...or perhaps nothing more than an extended complaint about the choice of a place to spend the day.

Ever since I told my wife Lyn about the scene, a new expression has been added to our verbal shorthand lexicon—you know, that code talk that every successful couple uses for quick communication. When one of us begins to belabor a point or argues too long on an issue, when further discussion is unnecessary...or pointless...the other one says, "Honk, honk, honk!"

As I have reflected upon that scene, numerous thoughts have occurred to me. There have been many times in my life when the honking was an important...even necessary...element in my learning experience—like when I was attempting to master riding the bicycle, or trying to perfect driving skills. I didn't always enjoy it, but it was often essential to my success.

There were the times when Mom or Dad honked relentlessly as their son gradually learned to sound out his words, and memorized his "tootums" (you know, tootums two is four, tootums four is eight, tootums eight is sixteen...*those* tootums), with much weeping and gnashing of teeth. Thankfully, their honking also often consisted of encouragement and praise.

My role as a husband and parent has varied between being the honker and the honkee. I'm certain that many times my fatherly advice and pronouncements translated to my children as endless honking aimed at making their lives miserable, and were often tuned out—much like the parents' voices in Charles Schultz's *Peanuts* TV cartoons, with their "Wah, wa wah-wah-wah."

My favorite insight about this insistent input, however, is that it is a reminder of the way the Lord has promised to guide all those who really want to please Him. Although His honking is almost never audible, He promised, "Thine ears shall hear a word behind thee, saying, 'This is the way, walk ye in it, when ye turn to the right hand, and when ye turn to the left.'" Isaiah 30:21

Parable of The Soup Pot

As an old advertising copywriter I can't help studying other hucksters' efforts to persuade the public to part with their dollars for some product or service they may or may not be able to live without. Sometimes the ads are clever but I can't remember the name of the product.

However, once in a while I see one that really does the job and makes me want to buy what they're promoting. The other day I saw one that really did that for me. The scene was a grocery store check-out line, with the clerk scanning a can of soup. Each time she scanned the can she got a different reading; "chicken" one time, "potatoes" the next, then "carrots," "noodles" and so on. Obviously chock-full of the best ingredients for good Chicken Noodle soup, right? Then the next lady in line drops a can of a leading brand of Chicken Noodle soup which rolls across the scanner. "Canned Soup" reads the scanner. How ordinary.

Well, that commercial hit the spot with me. This old ad man will surely look for that brand the next time I shop for Chicken Noodle soup. But at the same time it struck me for an entirely different reason. It reminded me of the vegetable soup my Mom used to make—and my wife still makes today—with its ingredients so bountiful you could eat it with a fork.

Before the days of vegetables commercially prepared for "home-made" soups, Mom cut, chopped, sliced and diced potatoes, tomatoes, carrots, okra, beans, corn, and just about anything else you can imagine, from scratch. She added the hand-trimmed chunks of beef and some water, put it all in the soup pot with just the right amount of salt and pepper and put it on the stove to stew. Before long the house was under the spell of that delightful, unmistakable aroma, which made the anticipation almost as satisfying as the partaking.

My dear wife goes Mom one better with her recipe, even though she does take advantage of the prepared vegetables much of the time, by including whatever vegetable leftovers are on hand. Ahhh, I love it. And it just gets better the longer it stays in the pot, although we usually consume it long before it reaches its potential peak flavor. It's just too good to wait for long.

There have been many times that I have used the illustration of that soup pot as a simile for the way Life works. We all start out like a pot of water, plus a few common, ordinary ingredients. All pretty much the same, right? But from that point on, the recipe is distinctively different for each one of us. Not only that, but it changes from day to day with each addition.

Just as there are all kinds of soups—some clear, some creamy; some eaten hot, others served cold; some are hearty entrees, some are tempting appetizers—there are infinite varieties of personalities, each one bearing the taste of its own combination of ingredients.

In the Divine soup recipes for us all there are no wasted experiences, no serendipitous events, no accidental occurrences that can spoil the "soup" that the Lord has planned to make of us. There is nothing that happens to us during a lifetime that He cannot use, either as a main character component, or, sometimes, simply to add a specific flavor to one's personality.

Oftentimes it is too easy for us to look over the Chef's shoulder and question why the ingredients we see spread out before us are necessary. We cry when the onions are chopped up. We find some herbs bitter and hard to swallow. This is too sweet. That's too salty. Or that's too spicy. And, ewww...that's too yucky. Not all of Life's events are fun...some, too painful.

We are too inclined to think in terms of the individual elements and events that touch our lives as separate and unrelated...each one to be chosen or rejected based upon its measure of pleasure or pain. God, however, has planned the perfect recipe for each of His own children, and, when we are done, He takes us off the fire and serves us up, the perfect soup. Bon appetit.

Parable of The Special Touch

It is one of the peculiar realities of life that oftentimes our "most embarrassing moments" provide some of the material that makes our existence more interesting. I proved that to myself recently while reminiscing with "Coot" Sewell at our North Fulton High School class reunion.

It was well into the B-team football game, being played in the North Fulton football stadium on a Saturday morning. I don't remember what the score was, but I do remember that we had the ball about mid-field, and that it was fourth and inches—and that Coach Maupin sent *me* in to play Center with instructions to run a quarterback sneak.

That might not seem significant to most people, but I was only second or third string Center and this was my time to shine—the coach, the team...the whole world (at least the cheerleaders and two or three dozen parents in the stands)...were watching. There was real potential for a Hero Moment ahead.

We all leaned in to the huddle as Coot called the play: "Quarterback sneak, on touch." We broke with a clap, turned and trotted manfully to the line of scrimmage, assuming the usual three-point stance with me straddling the ball and with Coot standing behind me.

After Coot surveyed the opposing team, like General Patton standing erect in his tank turret, he bent forward, placed his hands in the traditional position for receiving the ball, and ...

If the entire line, with Coot to boot, hadn't fallen on their faceguards in anticipation of the snapping of the ball, we would have been there still...with me waiting for Coot to say "Touch!" (Hey! How was I to know that "Touch" meant when I felt his hand touch my backside to receive the ball? Sure...like *you* knew! Well, it's easy to say that *now*, isn't it?)

I've come to a place in my life where I realize that we can learn a lot from those moments that only a few years ago we would have given anything to forget. For one thing, I seldom mistake *hearing* the word "touch" for the sensation of *feeling* a touch.

I learned that, however devastating the embarrassment may seem at the moment, people almost never "die of embarrassment." Our psyches may suffer painful bruises for awhile, but eventually we get over them and discover that embarrassment is seldom a terminal condition.

Another lesson to be gleaned from the embarrassments of life is that they are among the most effective means of keeping one's ego in check. Unless one is a professional stand-up comedian or writer—both of which often make successful careers out of joking and writing about their shortcomings—these little emotional setbacks can help avoid taking oneself too seriously.

I'm almost certain that Coot had long since forgotten about this traumatic event in my life. However, it has been one of my favorite personal anecdotes for all these years, and has been a perfect illustration of a great truth: All those old flaws and failings actually work together to make us what we will finally become...and, if properly kept in perspective, will make us more sympathetic and helpful to others as they experience their own humbling episodes.

This little tale also suggests something else to me—something that we all can take to heart as we try to muddle our way through Life's tangles and obstacles. It's not always easy to understand the instructions in Life's Owner's Manual; we spend a lot of time trying to interpret, translate, understand and apply even the simplest of guidelines for a joyful and productive life.

The fact is that life would be a lot easier if our Quarterback would just come up to us and say, "Touch!" when He was ready for us to do something. In reality, though, His communication is usually very subtle...an impression lightly placed upon our hearts...a "still, small voice," perhaps...or even a light and very special touch. Most often, that's the way I know He's there.

Parable of The Life Coach

When I was eleven years old and in the sixth grade at Park Street School in Marietta, Georgia, I was sure what I wanted to be when I grew up—a professional football coach. That was the year I signed up to play for the Marietta Baby Blue Devils, an elementary school team.

We had real uniforms and everything, including real football shoes with hard rubber cleats and the shoulder pads that made even the smallest of us look like an action hero. And it was all topped off with a gold helmet (our two coaches had played football for Georgia Tech).

Each day, as soon as school was out, my buddies and I would make our way over to the locker room in the basement of the Larry Bell Auditorium to get suited up. We did exercises to get loosened up...real calisthenics just like you saw the college and professional athletes doing in the newsreels at the Saturday movie matinee.

Our coaches taught us how to block, how to tackle...and how to avoid being blocked and tackled. We learned real football plays right out of the Georgia Tech playbook...all those X's and O's with the lines that showed the linemen where to block and the backs where to run. (I suppose that's why I've always liked football better than basketball and most of the other field sports—there was something more or less predictable about where you were supposed to be and what you were expected to do—except when the opposing X or O didn't cooperate.)

We depended on our coaches to tell us what positions we should play, what plays we would practice, what exercises and drills to do to improve our skills and physical condition. I wasn't especially fast, and only average height, so I was told to play guard...I guess coach thought I couldn't do too much harm with somebody on each side of me to help out.

I didn't disgrace myself playing for the Baby Blue Devils... even got my name in the local paper after a game with a team from Cartersville, Georgia. Although there *was* the time when I was honorary captain for a game, won the coin toss and chose to kick off because I liked to play defense—the coach shouted in his best "Dr. Phil" voice, "What were you thinking?! You always receive when you win the toss.!" That was my last time as honorary captain, as I recall.

Playing in an organized sport like that gives one a good picture of what life will be like: at every new stage there must be someone to show us what we are to do and how to do it...to keep an eye on us and make sure that we don't neglect "the basics"—of course, we all know that each endeavor has its own set of basic principles that must be observed for a successful result.

Sometimes our life coach is a parent, sometimes a sibling or a friend; often we are kept on the right track by a boss, a co-worker or a mentor. Our degree of progress and success often depends upon how faithful we are in responding to the instructions and encouragement...and sometimes the chastisement...meted out by that life coach, whoever he or she may be.

It is an inescapable fact that we each will also find ourselves cast in the role of life coach for someone else. That's when we pass on the life lessons learned from the coaches who have led us—sometimes kicking and screaming—through the portals of progress and accomplishment. And though we can instruct...whether as parent, spouse, boss or friend...only *they* can perform.

As a Believer, it is a great comfort to me to realize that God, the perfect coach, knows my abilities and potential; and, with that foreknowledge, has planned a path for me to follow, has ordained each experience to prepare me to get onto the field of life and participate up to the very limits of those abilities. And He promises to enable me to successfully follow His game plan.

Earthly life coaches must stand on the sidelines and watch, powerless, as their players perform. Only our Heavenly Coach can go onto the field with us and help us to the final victory.

Parable of The Turtle Shell

One of the main selling points for the house where we live was the comfortable, grandmother-style front porch. During the intervals when we are allowed to share it with the true owners, the bullying gangs of mosquitoes, it has brought us great joy.

Several years ago, several of the floor boards needed to be replaced, requiring me to get underneath to make some of the structural repairs. While I was under there, I made a discovery that did my grandfather heart good—I found the mostly-vacant shell of a small box turtle that had apparently become trapped inside the lattice work around the porch footings and expired.

Sir Turtle had been deceased for long enough that all the soft tissue was gone, leaving behind a perfect, complete skeleton, picked clean by the ants and other members of God's janitorial crew. The bottom plate of the shell had become detached, which allowed one to inspect what was inside, unlocking some of the secrets of turtledom.

For instance, I have always wondered what happened to the turtle's neck when he drew it in and pulled up the drawbridge against threats to his safety. Did you know that the turtle's neck is much like that of the owl—a long, S-curved extension of the spine, which can be run out and pulled back in with ease?

Or that the spine is built into the top of the shell, so that—contrary to what the cartoons would have us believe—the creature is permanently attached to the shell and can never come out? At least, not alive.

It was really fun to show the creature formerly known as Turtle to my grandchildren. And there were also a lot of grown-ups who were fascinated by what the friendly corpse revealed.

On top of everything else, that shell and the skeleton it contained were clear evidence that a turtle had lived...had once found its way under our porch. But the life essence, the indescribable element which *was* that turtle was no longer a part of what had been left behind.

You can observe the same thing on any beach—shells of mollusks and crustaceans—the former residents long since departed or picked out and eaten by someone higher up the food chain. Beachcombers spend hours seeking and discovering these treasures...evidence that many members of many species once dwelt in this territory that marks the joining of land and sea.

Each Easter season the media are filled with items that make me think of that humble turtle shell...and our collection of seashells, too...with their message to all who would learn: Life is short; and when it is finished often the only evidence of its existence is the empty shell that is left behind. Each year the Christian faithful gather to recollect the visit to the tomb that turned out to be empty, except for the only indication that Jesus had been there—the empty wrappings, still in the shape of His form.

Unlike the risen Savior, each of us will leave behind a physical "shell"...or husk, as my Dad was fond of saying. However, exactly like Jesus, that physical clue to our presence on earth will not be the only—or even the most important—proof of our life on earth.

On one of the walking trails in the Great Smokey Mountains National Park is a point where a large number of boxwood shrubs are growing wild—one of the last remaining signs of a family farm that occupied that spot a century or so ago. The family is gone... moved or long since deceased...but this once-loved garden is clear proof of their sojourn in that place.

Not only are believers assured that our souls—the essence, the personalities that are housed in our physical bodies—are immortal; but that our accomplishments, our influence on the lives of others, can be like that turtle shell...visible evidence of lives well lived and well spent.

Parable of The Jesus Lizard

Several years ago I learned about the Basilisk Lizard, of the species Basiliscus Basiliscus and Family Iguanidae. This extraordinary creature resides near rivers and streams in the rainforests of Central and South America.

As a member of the Iguana family, the Basilisk Lizard has all the usual defenses as its relatives: Outstanding camouflage, sharp claws, great quickness and running speed, and a tail which breaks away when grasped by an attacker, allowing the little guy to get away safely. That is a sufficient collection of defensive features to provide protection for most members of the family Iguanidae. Ah, but that doesn't tell the whole story of the Basilisk Lizard.

The Basilisk Lizard has a most unique trick for escaping all but the most agile and persistent of predators—one that has earned him an unusual nickname among his human rainforest neighbors: the Jesus Lizard. When pursued by one of his swift enemies, the speedy fellow rises on his back legs and runs to the nearest body of water. With flaps of skin between his rear toes for added surface area, and running at exactly the right speed, the canny creature runs across the surface of the water, leaving a wet and bewildered attacker to find an alternate entree for supper.

What made this particular species of lizard think that running across the surface of the water was a good idea? Did the first one to try it look like the cartoon character Wiley Coyote, who runs a few strides past the edge of a cliff, realizes his mistake, looks at the audience and says, "Oh-oh!" then falls to the valley floor with a puff of dust? Or, in the case of our lizard friend, sink to the bottom of the lake never to rise again?

In their denial of the possibility of an intelligent Creator, Evolution theorists would have us presume that numerous Basilisks tried the "walking on the water trick" unsuccessfully before one finally worked out the exact ratio of size to speed which would allow him to be supported by the surface tension of the body of water he was crossing. Too fast and the pressure of the running stroke would break surface tension...too slow and his weight would cause him to sink.

And, by the way, did he grow the additional flaps of skin between the toes of his back feet *before* he tried to tread water—when he had no need for them—or after? And does one decide to grow something like that? Certainly none of his species cousins had anything of the sort.

How many fossils of drowned lizards would it take to prove that they mastered this technique over a period of time? I would think it would take quite a few to provide convincing evidence. How many fossils have scientists found to prove their theory? None that I know of.

If the Jesus Lizard didn't learn his fabulous escape trick by trial and error, who do you think could have taught him? An Intelligent Creator, maybe? Why is that so hard to believe?

I don't know about you, but I can identify with Basiliscus Basiliscus. I could never count the times when I have found myself in a tight spot, with no obvious route of escape, only to feel moved to some sort of unlikely evasive action—not unlike trying to run away across the water.

So what are we to make of this Parable of the Jesus Lizard? I think it important that we recognize several things. First, we are the way we are not because of accident or trial and error, but because of a Creator Who designed us as unique beings with specific physical and mental abilities planned for the life He knew to be before us, and He left to us their discovery and use.

Second, He intended us to use those abilities without reservation...without a lot of questioning and analysis. Finally, He promises that when we are obedient He makes all that happens to us work "for our good if we love God and are fitting into His plans." Rom. 8:28 (LB)

Parable of The Believable Mr. Ripley

When I was a boy, one of my favorite features in the Atlanta newspaper, usually tucked off in one corner of the comics page, was "Believe It Or Not" by Robert Ripley. The intrepid Mr. Ripley traveled all over the world, seeking out strange, unusual—and often outlandish—tales and little-known facts, fables and foibles which he illustrated with line drawings.

Some of his items were more from the "Or Not" category, such as the one about the French military officer, I believe it was, who got part of his face shot away and, in the absence of a suitable skin graft, had the wound repaired with the only thing available...skin from the breast of a chicken. When the healing was complete, it was asserted that he grew a patch of feathers in the midst of his beard.

Well, after all, Mr. Ripley allowed us to "believe it or not," didn't he?

One of the somewhat more believable entries was accompanied by a drawing of a great stone table with a heavy round top. The illustration showed a channel clearly incised around the top, an inch or so from the edge.

As I recall, this was one of the few pieces of furniture in the tower cell where some famous nobleman was imprisoned. It is said that the gentleman, whether in misery or deep thought, was seen to walk round and round the table running his thumb along the table as he circled, like a human phonograph needle, until it eventually wore a groove an inch or so deep.

Now, that story sounds a little more believable, doesn't it? Especially when one compares it to real life experiences.

I have come to a place in my life where I realize how many otherwise impossible and unbelievable accomplishments yield to repetition, persistence and, sometimes, just plain cussedness. How many times have I given just one more twist on that immovable jar lid only to feel it begin to give way? Strained once more with the lug wrench before the nut came loose?

That's one of the things I learned from the entertaining, and mostly believable, Mr. Ripley. So many things in our earthly experience cannot be accomplished by the expenditure of an initial burst of energy and effort, or overcome by a wholesale headlong assault.

On the contrary, most of the great victories in life come as the result of an unwillingness to quit...a determination to follow through to the end, regardless of the difficulties encountered.

In 1916, when coach John Heisman's Georgia Tech team crushed hapless Cumberland College by the record-smashing score of 222-0, in what some called the "Little Big Horn" of football, one Atlanta sportswriter penned a line that captured what must be the attitude of all who would be victorious. He wrote, "Each goal was the culmination of a sustained drive."

When faced with a physical or mental challenge...one that seems beyond my ability to overcome...I have learned to hang on a little longer, keep trying a little harder, in short, not to quit—at least not yet. It is the effort that occurs after most people quit that often wins the victory.

I remember a statistic that shows that most sales are made by less than twenty percent of salesmen. About half of all salesmen make one or two sales calls on a prospect and quit. Another third make four or five sales calls and quit. Less than twenty percent of salesmen make six or more sales calls on a prospect—and they are responsible for eighty percent of the sales!

Whatever one's goal in life...whether removing a jar lid or displacing a boulder, solving a mental exercise or dealing with a social difficulty...we can all take a tip from the believable Mr. Ripley. Continuous, persistent effort can accomplish astonishing things. Many, if not all, of life's victories prove to be the culmination of a sustained drive...a "don't-know-when-to-quit."

Parable of The Wrong Goal

As a native of Atlanta, Georgia, and a graduate of Georgia Tech, I have known the story of Roy "Wrong Way" Riegels since I was a little boy. It was the 1929 Rose Bowl when Georgia Tech won over the California Bears, largely because of a minor directional error on his part.

When Stumpy Thomason of Tech lost the ball after a tackle by Cal's Benny Lom, Riegels gathered up the ball and started for the Tech goal. However, in his effort to elude tacklers he got turned around a time or two, and, according to Riegels, "I completely lost my bearings."

As Riegels raced down the field—toward the California goal—his teammates valiantly sprinted to catch him...while Tech players tried to block them all the way. Lom finally caught and stopped his friend on the one yard line, where the Yellow Jacket players swarmed him. Cal's subsequent punt was blocked out of the end zone for a safety. Tech won the game 8-7.

And what fan of American aviation history can ever forget the story of that other "Wrong Way"? Douglas "Wrong Way" Corrigan.

As a young man, Corrigan helped build the Spirit of Saint Louis, the airplane flown non-stop across the Atlantic Ocean by Charles Lindbergh. Inspired by Lindbergh's success, Corrigan dreamed of making his own transatlantic flight. He was of Irish decent, so he chose Ireland as his intended destination. However, federal authorities refused permission for such a flight, saying that, although sound enough for cross-country flights, Corrigan's airplane was not suitable for non-stop transatlantic travel.

On July 17, 1938, Corrigan took off in heavy fog from Floyd Bennett Field in Brooklyn, New York—supposedly for a return cross-country flight to California—and flew for twenty-six hours through poor visibility, using only his magnetic compass for direction. He asserted that when he dropped below the clouds he found himself over a large body of water...and then discovered he had been "following the wrong end of the magnetic needle." A couple of hours later, he landed at Baldonnel Airport in Dublin.

Despite attempts by authorities to get him to admit he had made the flight illegally, Wrong Way stuck by his explanation. "That's my story," he maintained, and never wavered.

My Dad grew up with a close friend who began as a youth grooming himself for success. He would stand in front of a full-length mirror practicing introducing himself, smiling, engaging himself in social conversation. He was a leader in the church youth group and in high school organizations. He once confided to Dad that his goal was to retire at age fifty with half a million dollars in the bank. That was a substantial retirement fund in 1920's dollars.

Dad was present in the hospital room with this man years later, as someone steadied his hand so he could sign the contract that would later prove to put his net worth over $500,000. He was only weeks away from his fiftieth birthday—but he never made it. His family was last heard quarreling bitterly over how the estate should be divided and who was entitled to what.

Three men with three distinct goals. Two of them will forever be footnotes in history books because they flew toward the wrong goals—one with misguided zeal, the other with guile that prevented him from freely enjoying the significance of his accomplishment. The third man, who spent his entire life pursuing a material goal, died with his goal just beyond his grasp.

Someone once remarked that one of the saddest stories in life is to complete the climb up the ladder of success, only to find the ladder leaning against the wrong wall...and to realize that one didn't even enjoy the climb. Jesus advised us to "Seek ye first the kingdom of God and His righteousness and all these *things* will be added unto you." That is the only goal with a promise.

Parable of The Un-Question

It's called a rhetorical question. When my mother's remarkably keen ear caught my sassy response, muttered under my breath as I sullenly retreated following my most recently earned "rearing," she exploded, "WHAT did you SAY?!"

Dear reader, don't misinterpret that as an inquiry into sentence structure, depth of meaning, or choice of vocabulary. She knew what I said, all right—or, at least, recognized the rebellion cloaked by those unintelligible sounds—and she wasn't going to put up with it.

When my dad casually asked me during one Sunday dinner, "Son, do you know how that front bumper got dented?" It wasn't dented on Saturday afternoon—before I drove the family chariot on a date. Now it had a distinctive, new crease that was difficult to overlook...no matter how much I tried. "What dent?" I asked, rhetorically.

(Let's see...nice shiny, sound bumper...Jack drives on a date... scraped, dented bumper. Hmmmmm.) Now, Dad knew there was no destructive Bumper Fairy roaming the countryside. I'm satisfied that he had a pretty good idea of the answer to his question, just as Mom did to hers (and, to tell the truth, just as I knew which dent).

These kinds of questions are the stock in trade of all parents...in fact, of just about every authority figure. Sometimes their intention is to focus on a problem...sometimes they serve to generate thought or make a point. And only occasionally is the answer important.

At times the only purpose of such questions is sarcasm. "Where do you think you're going, to a fire?" "Do you call that noise, music?" "If Johnny stuck his head in the fire, would you?" "What were you thinking?" "Where are you going in that outfit, a tacky party?" Some questions, such as, "Does this dress make me look too fat?" are too deep to be satisfied by the most obvious, simple answers.

When God asked Adam and Eve, "Where are you?" the answer had nothing to do with geography. Nor when He queried Cain, asking, "Where is your brother?" was He seeking the solution to a problem in global positioning. And they knew it. Just look at their answers.

Adam didn't say, "Over here behind the persimmon tree, in the plum thicket." Cain didn't respond, "Gee, Lord, the last time I saw him he was out in the south forty." No, as Jesus said in one of His parables, "They began with one accord to make excuse." And, as my mother used to say, you don't start making excuses unless you know you've done something wrong.

There is a rule observed by all good trial lawyers: Never ask a witness a question to which you don't already know the answer. That's the way it is with the Lord's interrogations. Our Omniscient God is never surprised, shocked or dismayed by our answers to His questions.

The amazing fact is that He bothers to question us at all. That is a testimony to His love, patience and readiness to extend to us His gift of gracious forgiveness.

So, when you find yourself under the probing searchlight of His divine interrogation, you might just as well surrender to it. No artfully constructed defense...no airtight alibi...no skillfully articulated excuse will alter the justice of His judgment.

But for all who seek to please Him, His pronouncements are nothing to fear. After all, He is the originator of the gentle words, "Be not afraid, neither be dismayed."

The rest of that passage in the book of Joshua reads, "For the Lord thy God is with thee whithersoever thou goest." And because He was with us, He is already aware of the correct answers to His probing questions...He is simply allowing us the opportunity to face up to our responsibility for our actions. That confession permits us to receive the loving grace He offers.

Parable of The Last Chance

I have suffered from an annoying, and often embarrassing, condition most of my life. Although it isn't as overwhelming as it once was...and I'm better able to manage it than I used to be...it still affects my life and relationships in many ways.

It's not what you might suspect—not some dreadful disease or physical disability...not a deeply seated psychological disorder. It is just that I have always had a very relaxed attitude towards time. Whereas many people go through life racing the clock, and others show an utter disdain for it, I have experienced a friendly fellowship with time. You might call it a peaceful coexistence with the clock.

When I was a boy living at home, this used to drive my dad crazy. He was a classic Type A personality, whose motto was, "It's better to be thirty minutes early than thirty seconds late."

One of my most vivid memories is of him pacing back and forth by the front door, ready to go, checking his watch and loudly singing, over and over, the chorus from a popular Country song of the day, "I'm waiting, waiting in the lobby of your heart ...". My tendency towards tardiness once moved him to chide me in frustration, "Son, when you finally arrive in heaven, the song they'll be singing is, 'When the *rolls are cold* up yonder, I'll be there.'!"

I'm a lot better than I used to be, but I still tend to operate in accordance with "Just In Time" theory. (That's a management theory based on the idea that it is a waste of resources to have them on hand a minute before they are needed.) I frequently find myself with no time to spare...no contingency plan...often leaving things unfinished—or un-begun—in order to meet whatever schedule happens to be tyrannizing me at the moment.

Thankfully, however, the Lord, in His grace, has allowed me to get the important things done, and has protected me from the regret that results from missing the last opportunity to do the really important things. As a young man, a lot of my actions and responses were governed by the question, "If this person only saw me this one time, would he believe that I'm a Christian—and would that be good or bad?" Nowadays I tend to ask myself, "If this was the last time this person and I saw each other, what kind of a memory would it be for each of us?"

I was the last person to talk to my mother this side of the Kingdom. I'm sure it was the inspiration of the Spirit that moved me to call at that hour on a Saturday night. We had a nice conversation, and as we finished she told me, as she often did, "I like it when you call...you make me laugh." Before she awoke next morning she suffered the stroke that took her away.

I had several long conversations with my dad within hours before his damaged heart finally gave out. I reminded him of one of his favorite verses: "Wait on the Lord; be of good courage, and He shall strengthen thine heart. Wait, I say, on the Lord." (Psalm 27:14)

I've written before about Dad's last hours, and the fact that his last words before meeting Jesus face to face, were to ask the attending nurse if she knew Jesus. Faithful to what he taught in 125

Lay Evangelism Schools in Baptist churches around the country, his last conscious act was one of concern for the spiritual condition of those around him. Faithful, indeed, to the last.

I take comfort, and find encouragement, in the example of Jesus, Who is never seen to be in a hurry as He goes from place to place; always dealing with each person as if he or she was the only one around, taking all the time needed to deal with their need.

Jesus' example also convicts me, because He was always exactly on time—never early, never late. His Spirit ministers to my needs in the same way, and alerts me to opportunities to demonstrate His love and grace to those around me as if it would be my last chance. It may be.

Parable of The Near Miss

Many of my favorite memories have to do with trips taken in the family automobile. I remember with fondness the car packed with kids and their stuff, rolling down the highway—and the sights and sounds of travel. I can recall the sound of my parents singing...my girls playing.

And, of course, whether I was one of the kids or one of the adults, I remember the travel sound that pushes grown-ups everywhere to the very brink of sanity: "Are we there yet?" And, then, there are its most common variations: "Is it much farther?" and "How much longer ...?"

It may seem strange, but those images of traveling with children were what occurred to me the other day while reading a familiar story from the Bible.

Mark 12:28-34 is a favorite passage, read, underlined and marked with comments in many of the Bible translations I've accumulated over many years of studying and teaching Sunday School. Even so, every time I come across it I find some new truth or application. After all, the Bible is a living book, constantly offering new views of the Lord's plan for our lives.

In the passage, a man of the law asks Jesus which is the most important commandment. In the NIV, it reads, "When Jesus saw that he had answered wisely, he said to him, 'You are not far from the kingdom of God.' And from then on no one dared ask Him any more questions."

Now...here's what came to me. The lawyer asked which was the greatest, the most important, commandment—if one only focused on one of the laws in an attempt to be an obedient servant, which one should it be? There are two reasons for obeying the laws of a nation. One is merely to avoid the penalties for disobedience; the other is to demonstrate that one is a law-abiding citizen of that nation.

When Jesus told the man, "You are not far...", He wasn't implying that the man was already qualified as a citizen of the Kingdom. If that's what He meant, He would have said so. Therefore, the keeping of these two, most important, commandments isn't enough to qualify one for citizenship in the Kingdom of God. Near, perhaps...not far, yes...but not there yet.

There are traditionally only two ways to become a citizen of a kingdom or a country. Either by birth or through the legal process called naturalization, whereby one performs certain acts of loyalty to the new nation while renouncing loyalty to all other authorities and nations. Abiding by the laws is not enough—only full compliance to the naturalization process will do.

The news is full of reports of "illegal aliens," people who enter a country without going through the proper legal channels. No matter how sincere their motives for coming, they have no rights afforded to citizens under our legal system. Even legal aliens find that their rights and protections under the law are definitely limited. Only citizens can expect full protection.

Jesus is the only man who was naturally born as a citizen of the Kingdom of God. All the rest of us can only become naturalized citizens through the process Jesus called being born again. We demonstrate our new relationship by being obedient to the laws of the Kingdom...and we can only do that by keeping them always before us. The Bible tells us that only the Spirit can give us the desire—and the ability—to be obedient to the Kingdom laws.

The lawyer wasn't far from the Kingdom...but he was merely an illegal alien who could not expect the benefits of abiding by the law. One must meet the conditions for citizenship, and keep one's eyes on the only One Who could keep him as a secure citizen, for that to be possible.

Believers are pilgrims, sojourners and strangers in this world; but we are full-fledged citizens of the Kingdom of God. Does your citizenship lie in the Kingdom? Are you there yet, or are you "not far"? Remember..."not far" has still not arrived—and a near miss is still a miss.

Parable of The Not Dead

I have a confession to make: I have long been a fan of the British comedy series "Monty Python's Flying Circus." It is very British, frequently risque, often irreverent—though not overly so—sometimes just plain silly...but for the most part I find it to be hilariously entertaining.

One of the Monty Python products that I have laughed at many times is the movie titled "Monty Python and the Holy Grail." (I have to be careful how I talk about this, because I have many friends and acquaintances who simply wouldn't understand—either because they don't quite get the British style of humor, or because they tend to be too Pharisaical about some of the language and premises. And they might be right. But I can't help it...thinking about it really cheers me up and makes me chuckle.)

One scene takes place in a squalid, medieval village, as the peasants deal with hapless victims of the Plague. As a cart is pulled through the muddy street, one person bangs a gong and shouts, "Bring out your dead!" Bodies are unceremoniously swung onto the cart's disorderly pile. Sounds ghastly, doesn't it? One almost wants to apologize for laughing out loud at the comic action as the scene unfolds.

At one point, a not-quite-lifeless victim is brought to the cart, struggling weakly and saying, "I'm not dead." The person carrying him argues, "You almost are." "But I'm getting better," asserts the unwilling un-corpse. In the Broadway musical version of "Holy

Grail," this character is called Not Dead Fred, and he has a song of his own which he performs in a lively manner. And he appears in several more scenes, all of which proves that he is, indeed, not dead.

I heard a devotional today that reminded me of Not Dead Fred and his struggle to climb off the funeral pile. The speaker referred to a message by her new, young pastor, who began a recent sermon with the question, "Are you dead yet?"

The pastor structured his sermon around Paul's teaching that we are to be dead to sin and raised to new life in Christ. In that context, the character of Not Dead Fred becomes one that is all too familiar. In fact, he begins to look a lot like me at a number of critical stages in my life.

There have been plenty of times when I was deeply convicted of my failure to do those things which please God, those things required by Him of those who believe in and follow Him. The Holy Spirit waits patiently for me to climb onto the cart of those dead to sin...then, before I make that most important decision of one's life, I begin to think of some of those sin-things that I'm about to give up, and start thinking that, perhaps, I'm getting better. Nope, I'm not dead yet. At least to those few new, sinful things. Maybe later. And I have replayed this scene too often.

Haven't we all at some time or other volunteered to "make our bodies a living sacrifice" to God, only to have second thoughts, and felt reluctant to make such a final decision, and tried to crawl off the altar while there was still opportunity? No, I haven't been snooping into your personal life, but I'm certain that I'm not the only one that has felt that way at times during my life. After all, volunteering as a living sacrifice isn't easy—it takes an uncommon commitment.

I don't identify spiritually with Not Dead Fred these days. It's true that my sin reflex still takes control at times, somewhat like the occasional corpse in the morgue that sits upright under its covering as a result of rigor mortis. And I may not be the *first* to hop onto the cart carrying home those who are dead to sin. But I have learned not to be so quick to run away...or struggle so vigorously with the Spirit ...or expend so much effort trying to scramble off the sacrificial altar. I'm much more willing to die to each day's new sin.

So...tell me. Are YOU dead yet?

Parable of The One In Charge

"I don't know what you mean by 'Glory'," Alice said.
Humpty Dumpty smiled: "I meant 'there's a nice, knock-down argument for you'."
"But 'Glory' doesn't mean 'a nice, knock-down argument'," Alice objected.
"When I use a word," Humpty Dumpty said, "it means exactly what I choose it to mean, neither more nor less."
"The question is," said Alice, "whether you can make words mean so many different things."
"The question is," said Humpty Dumpty," which is to be master, that's all."
Alice Through the Looking Glass — Lewis Carroll

I've loved that quotation since I first came across it as a young reader. And the question it poses is an important one when you think about it: Which is master, the word or the word-monger? Which *should* be in charge?

One of my early voice teachers got sidetracked (as he often did during voice lessons) while teaching about the importance of voice control. He said that if one can control one's voice it is then a simple matter to control one's emotions.

He observed that most people...when angry, frustrated, excited, frightened—in fact, when under almost any kind of stress...reveal their mental condition through their manner of speaking. Their speech rhythm becomes more rapid, their vocal pitch climbs higher, their volume increases to greater decibel levels.

Not all signs will necessarily become obvious at once, but, as the degree of agitation increases, they all merge, surging to a climactic peak, giving fair warning to even a casual observer to back away, because the breaking point is near.

We've all seen those disaster movies, where the camera keeps cutting to the scene of the panicked operator who watches as the needle on the pressure gauge approaches the red "Caution" mark. Finally, in terror, he shouts, "Run for it boys! She's gonna blow!"

I learned a life-altering lesson about these three signs—tempo, pitch and volume. They aren't just gauges of emotions. They're not merely like thermometers which factually reveal and record one's mental and psychological condition in real time. If that was their only function, they would still be useful tools in dealing with people. But they're much more versatile than that.

These three vocal cues also have the unique capacity to serve as thermostats. In other words, they can not only register the fact of one's emotional state, but can actually enable one to alter and control those emotions...all with the simple tactic of speaking more slowly, more softly and at a lower pitch. Try it next time you're angry, or in a panic. I guarantee that it works.

Even while they were quite young, our girls learned to interpret my moods by listening to me talk. When they heard me talking softly, slowly and in my deepest basso voice, they knew that someone was hip deep in prunes. They recognized that I was adjusting my emotional thermostat, and they didn't rest easily until my tempo, pitch and volume returned to normal.

Another fascinating feature of this phenomenon is that it also works in reverse. When circumstances call for intense, forceful response, just gradually begin to talk louder, speak faster and in a higher register, and...voila! Bystanders will either respond to the voice of authority or begin to shift into "fight or flight" mode in preparation for the expected explosion.

Not only that, but while applying the three mysterious controls in order to *appear* to be in control, we actually can bring ourselves under control. Whether restraint or action is called for, the wise use of tempo, pitch and volume is the key to controlling emotions, to being in charge.

The loving Creator designed us with this ability to live our lives not as thermometers, but as thermostats, mastering circumstances, enabling us to be the ones in charge. Praise His name.

Parable of The Distant Spot

For someone who never served in the military, I spent a lot of my adolescence in uniform. I was in high school and college during the days of the Cold War, when most young men were required, or expected, to take training in the ROTC—Reserve Officers Training Corps—or some acceptable substitute.

As a high school Freshman my first ROTC assignment was as platoon guide. That's the fellow who is always located at the right front of the platoon on the drill field, and when marching in close order drill formation his job is to lead them in a straight course down the field.

I took my responsibility seriously and was intent upon keeping on line. And in order to do that I quickly learned not to look at the ground ahead, but to pick an object at the distant end of the drill field and steer steadily toward it.

That's the same principle applied by a farmer plowing his field. Whether walking purposefully behind a mule or perched high upon his modern machinery, the idea is identical—pick a distant spot and make a straight course to it, without looking down or turning back.

Ballet dancers pirouette and whirl, taking turns around the stage, without becoming dizzy or losing their direction. They can do that with precision, because at the rear of the theater there is always a point of light for them to see and focus upon—they call that act "spotting."

I remember being told that the best way to avoid the headaches and queasy feelings of car sickness is to look outside the automobile for a while, instead of trying to focus on the unsteady, jostling interior. I've tried that, and it really works. After all, the driver seldom gets car sick.

These images came to mind recently when a young friend was telling me about the discouragement he was experiencing as a result of a series of setbacks he had encountered. Work, finances, sick children, maintenance problems with his house and automobile... all seemed to be pressing in on him to a disturbing degree, and all at once. Each problem was more urgent than the one before, and he just couldn't make headway in dealing with any of them.

As I listened, it occurred to me that I had felt the same way many times during my life. I suspect that most of us spend a great deal of our lives looking at our feet...looking at those worrisome, pesky details that threaten to trip us up...when we ought to have our heads up, looking to that distant spot that is placed so as to keep us in balance and on a straight course.

I find a hint of this idea of focusing on that distant spot in Hebrews 12:1. "Let us throw off everything that hinders and the sin that so easily entangles, and let us run with perseverance the race marked out for us. Let us fix our eyes on Jesus ..." (NIV)

I'm convinced the adversary wants us to look at our feet, at those things that would throw us off-stride, off balance and off course. The Lord urges us to look to Jesus...that distant Spot...while He makes our path straight, our step firm, our success sure. What a blessed assurance!

Parable of The Quiet Call

In thirty or so years of teaching Sunday School, I know I have spent a considerable amount of time on the subject of one's calling. How and when God called characters in the Bible —the nature of the tasks to which they were called—make fascinating studies. How those illustrations apply to contemporary lives can be even more exciting and challenging.

I grew up in the South, in what one humorist called the "buckle of the Bible belt," and spent a lot of time in churches where the occasional "Testimony Time" was a common occurrence. You know... that's where individuals are encouraged to stand up and tell what the Lord has done for them lately. It seems that most folks are too sophisticated for that kind of emotional service these days. It takes an involvement many modern worshipers prefer to avoid.

In those services you were likely to hear anything from a dramatic "gutter to glory" salvation experience, to a tale of miraculous healing, to a story of needs providentially met. Sometimes there was tempting gossip fodder. I usually sat through those times in more or less awkward silence—the Lord just didn't seem to do things in my life in such spectacular ways.

Like many church goers I know, I was baptized and joined the church as a young person, long before I had the inclination or opportunity to commit any of the big, juicy sins. It's hard to sensationalize the distinction between sinner and saved at age twelve. So I kept quiet.

Perhaps that's why it is often difficult for today's readers to identify with those biblical callings. After all, how many folks do you know who have experienced one of those "burning bush, blinding light from above, voice from heaven" moments? Even the soft whisper of "This is the way, walk in it" is a rare—and most often nonexistent—occurrence for most of us.

So...can we say God still directly calls individuals today? I'm convinced from my own experience that He most assuredly does. However...in my life, at least...those calls were most often in the form of a door ajar, a beckoning fork in the trail, even an accidental wrong turn.

Believers can often recognize His influence in a chance to move in a particular direction ...in a particular type of activity...to interact with a nearby individual. If one had planned those things, and waited until prepared for them, the experience of God's call might have been missed.

As I replay my life on the picture screen inside my forehead, I recognize ample evidence of the Lord's quiet calling. In contrast, I can't seem to find a single burning bush, blinding light experience that influenced my actions. Most of my accomplishments have resulted from my unconscious response to barely discernable urging of the Holy Spirit—whispers, not loud calls.

I love music. I have participated in many school, church and community groups as soloist, chorus member, and leader. However, none of those opportunities ever came to me as a result of my effort—I have never been selected to perform as the result of an audition...never.

Except for my first job out of college, I have never received an offer of a job for which I had made an application. Even during that two year period I characterize as being "available for immediate employment." If that were the whole story it would be just too sad for words, right?

The truth is that through all my failed efforts to promote and provide for myself, make my own breaks, carve my own way, the Lord has continually proved that He had a better plan. What He leads me to—quietly calls me to—is always better suited to the talents and abilities that He programmed into my nature than the things to which I have aspired.

The Spirit promise is to be with us, continuing to guide, to direct, to urge us on in unrestrained response to each new call. And when I respond to that quiet, but urgent call, I find that I am seldom tempted to the delusion that I am in control of my life. Nor that I need to be.

Parable of The Falling Rain

One of my dad's favorite recordings when I was a boy was "Into Each Life Some Rain Must Fall," by a quartet called The Ink Spots. If you are old enough to remember The Ink Spots you can also remember the days of 78 RPM records, days when songs were recorded on these heavy discs about 10 inches in diameter, with only one song per side.

Before the days of High Fidelity recording equipment and techniques, those old 78's were clumsy things. They were easy to break and the grooves scratched easily. The sound was shallow and tinny-sounding, and listening to them was usually like hearing a concert while standing in the shower with the water turned on full blast. But to a boy it was still wonderful.

That song by The Ink Spots got played over and over. I still remember Dad singing along. "Into each life some rain must fall, but too much has fallen in mine. Into each heart some tears must come, but some day the sun will shine."

This all came back to me recently during a sermon about the importance of maintaining a strong church relationship. I believe the scripture reference was the one about building a house on solid rock instead of on the sand. You know, where it says "... and the rains descended and the floods came ...". And into each life some rain must fall ...

(Bless the pastor's heart, he did his best to make his point—and I'm sure he accomplished it with most of the folks—but my mind was off again on a mental cross-country expedition, free-lancing thoughts and messages that I was unable to bring under control.)

The importance of a strong foundation is exactly to protect us when the rains descend, the floods come and the winds blow. There will come times when circumstances will overwhelm us if we haven't taken the time to develop a solid foundation.

"Why do I need to learn *this* stuff? I'll never use this as a (fill in a career)." Every parent, every teacher has been confronted by a frustrated student or angry child with this question. Or at least with the attitude it represents. I've asked it myself on many occasions. I guess we all have.

I wish I could tell you how many times I have tried to impress the point that the whole point of any educational process is to provide us with a basic arsenal of facts and principles to be used in confronting and solving the problems that the storms of Life will rain upon us. Each thing one learns makes it possible to learn the next thing. Each thing one learns is an additional foundation stone upon which one's life will ultimately stand.

Recently I read that "All things are inexplicable...until someone explicates them to you." I wish I could explicate how delightful it is to learn new things...how much joy there is in the discovery of how to apply those things newly learned to unravel the puzzles of daily life.

Perhaps it is enough to stress that, since God never wastes anything, it is entirely consistent with His nature to believe that He has a useful purpose for each experience we face... that He intends for us to use these experiences as raw material to prepare us for the work He has in His mind for us to undertake. Some things apply directly... some are just for our enjoyment.

Children who were dragged "kicking and screaming" through the portals of learning will one day reach a point where, as adults, they either express gratitude for the learning experience or regret that they regarded it with such distaste. If only someone had explicated more clearly.

Sooner or later, the falling rain, the coming of floods, the irresistible blowing of the wind, will reveal two things: 1) How wisely we selected our life's building site. 2) How diligently we selected and placed the foundation stones upon which our life was to be built. Then may we be able to sing, "Into my life some rain did fall, but my foundation held up just fine."

Parable of The Steeple

Not too many years ago, I was helping my church in Atlanta develop materials for a program designed to inspire church members to become involved in evangelistic visitation. One of the ideas was centered on the thought of learning how to point people to the cross.

The Minister of Education—a former radio announcer—was making a videotape for that purpose and had assembled a series of visual images that illustrated his moving message nicely. As happens so often, though, things didn't work out as he had planned.

The big climax he had in mind was to emphasize our church as the focus point for those wanting to respond to the message of the Cross. As his narration and the music track built to a dramatic climax, the visual image on screen was of our church's steeple.

By the way, that steeple is familiar and well known to Atlanta natives, especially those from Northwest Atlanta. It is an impressive, exact reproduction of a Christopher Wren steeple, copied from the historic First Baptist Church in Providence, Rhode Island.

During a period when Atlanta was emerging as a major hub for the airline industry—and long before the age of all the electronic navigational gadgets—pilots often told of flying into and out of Atlanta and using that steeple as a major landmark in aligning their approach to, and departure from, the Atlanta airport.

Anyway...try to imagine the setting...the resonant voice of the narrator increasing in intensity as he reaches the stirring conclusion, the background music beginning to swell as it approaches the final phrases of the song "People Need the Lord"...while the camera majestically climbs the stately steeple, zooming in at last on its crowning element—the...*weathervane?* Not the expected cross, but a weathervane! No doubt a Christian weathervane, but a weathervane, none the less. You just have to imagine the picture, because, as you might guess, it never made it into the finished production.

Discovering that weathervane dealt quite a blow to my image of my church. From its very beginning, that church has been the spiritual home of many of the movers and shakers of Atlanta and Georgia. Among its members have been counted numerous leaders of commerce, Presidents and Board Chairmen of some of the nation's most powerful companies; legislators, governors and former governors; federal, state and local judges; leading educators, including at least one college president; even an Attorney General of the United States.

For most of the Twentieth Century, that church was a respected leader among the churches of the Southern Baptist Convention, its pastors active and effective during the days of the Atlanta Civil Rights struggles. Many of its members had been called to both the foreign and home mission fields...in fact, at that time, one-half of its budget was designated for missions.

Maybe you can understand why I was so disappointed by that vision of our steeple's crest. Here's why: The biblical ideal for my church, indeed, any church, is that it hold up a firm, unchanging standard to the world as represented by the Cross of Christ, pointing the way to God.

With all due respect to Sir Christopher Wren, a weathervane is absolute only in its ability to yield to the pressures of whatever wind happens to be blowing. It doesn't exemplify the kind of spiritual, moral and ethical leadership one would hope to find valued by a body of Believers.

Jesus said that His followers *are* salt...affecting the flavor of life. He said we *are* light... illuminating the obstacles in life. He said we are like cities on a hill...our steeple light should attract the weary and hopeless to a place where they can find peace, hope, joy and comfort. If all we offer is a commentary on the state of things, we've no more purpose than that weathervane.

Parable of The Appointed Time

"How long can you hold your breath?"

I've asked that question at least twice in the last couple of months while talking to people about their concern for the future. Neither was in dire straits, but they were each struggling with thoughts of how to provide for their families and at the same time find satisfaction in their work.

I've observed that one of the comforts of being within sight of "old buzzard-hood" is the ability to look over one's shoulder at the accumulation of life experiences and spot those times when I felt the same concerns, anxieties, and, yes, outright fears, and identify the many and diverse ways I was brought through them all.

Through greater and lesser trials...and also a reasonable number of modest successes...struggling to drag a business career, kicking and screaming, through the portals of financial and professional success, there have been plenty of times when the future was uncertain, my goals unclear and my prognosis for success unexciting.

During just such a period as that, I happened to be teaching an adult Sunday School class a lesson on the story of the prophet Jonah. That study, and the insights I have gained since that time, taught me a lesson that has proved to be a source of faithful patience and increased endurance that has been a constant inspiration to me—and the well-spring for encouragement that I have been able to share by the dipper-full with others like my two young friends.

Whenever I am tempted to doubt my resources...and occasionally, I have to admit, when I have questioned my Lord's desire to help me out of some disagreeable situation...I ask myself—as I asked my friends—"How long can you hold your breath?"

You see, when Jonah was aboard the storm-tossed ship and realized that his disobedience was endangering the safety of his unsuspecting shipmates, he told them to throw him into the treacherous sea in order to relieve themselves of the threat of God's wrath. Reluctantly they took his advice, threw him into the roiling waves and praised God as the storm ceased.

Meanwhile, as Jonah sank into the deep, *holding his breath*, the Biblical narrative continues, "Now the Lord prepared a great fish to swallow up Jonah ..." Here's where the story really caught my imagination.

The word in the King James Version that is translated "prepared" comes from a Hebrew word that, according to one Concordance, can also be translated "appointed." As a businessman I can identify with the word Appointed—more than the word Prepared. Appointments imply planning, intent, preparation, commitment, faithfulness, dependability.

My Dad always tried to impress on me as a young salesman that when you make an appointment you were duty-bound to be there on time and ready to do business. So, when I saw the word Appointed I began to do a bit of research.

I'm not a marine biologist by any means, so forgive me if I misstate the facts, but here is the way I understand the situation. The Mediterranean Sea doesn't naturally contain non-carnivorous fish of sufficient size to swallow a man whole. The Whale Shark is big enough, but it is native to the Indian Ocean. The Great White Shark is big enough, too, but it would be more likely to swallow him in bite-sized morsels. Many members of the Whale family would do, but the nearest ones abide in the waters of the Atlantic Ocean. But the *Lord* appointed ...

For the sake of argument, let's rule out the Whale Shark from the Indian Ocean, and the Great White, with its propensity to think of mankind in terms of appetizers and entrees. The most likely resource for the Lord to commission would then be one of the great whales from the Atlantic Ocean, don't you think? So the Lord set up an appointment. So far, so good. Right?

Let's recap: Jonah is under water, still sinking like a stone, holding his breath. Now, where is that great fish? But the Lord set the appointment, and He is never late—never early, either, but absolutely never late. So at some point in the Lord's time, He located a great fish; He gave that fish the urge to go to a place that wasn't its normal habitat, crossing several hundred miles of open sea, traveling to the east on a specific latitude to arrive at a particular longitude.

Do you know the cruising speed of a great fish? I'm sure I don't, but I do know that it took some time to cross from the Atlantic through the Mediterranean. And I know that the Lord inspired that fish to depart at such a time, and swim at such a speed, toward exactly the correct coordinates so that it would arrive precisely on time. The Lord always keeps His appointments.

So...there's Jonah, still holding his breath; probably rethinking his rebellion, and his impulsive suggestion that he be thrown into the sea. When, suddenly, this great creature approaches, its maw gaping wide, taking in everything in its path, including the debris from Jonah's former ship, no doubt...and Jonah as well.

Is the Lord surprised by our rebellion? Perplexed by the problems that confront those of us who are faithful to Him? Undecided about how to assist us in our difficulties? Not a bit.

Almost certainly, days—maybe weeks—before Jonah decided to disobey His order to go witness to Nineveh, the Lord had already picked out His candidate for Great Fish Hero of the Month, programmed it with the proper GPS (God's Positioning System) coordinates, set its internal chronometer and cruise control to make its appointment before Jonah's breath ran out.

Think you have problems, situations you can't handle, financial or health issues that are about to overwhelm you? If you love the Lord and want to please Him, be assured that He has appointed a great fish for you. Take a deep breath and hold it as a reminder that it will be enough. He knows how long you can hold out...and your fish will arrive right on time.

If you don't know Him, but could really use a great fish about now, just let me know. I'll be glad to show you how to set up an appointment. But don't put it off if you want that fish to show up before *you* run out of breath.

Parable of The Saturday Project

"I have a project for you when you get a chance," came the call from the kitchen.

I don't know about you, but there aren't many opening declarations that gather dark clouds of despair faster than that one. Don't get me wrong. I love my wife dearly, and there is not a thing that I wouldn't gladly try to provide her. She knows I really want to please her.

It's the idea of a Saturday project that's the problem. For in the folklore of our family my Saturday projects read like the trials of Hercules, or the challenges of Beowulf. The minute I lay hands on it, even the simplest and most straightforward of tasks has the ability to transmorgrify (think "Transformers") into the most complex and convoluted undertaking imaginable.

Last weekend was a good example. The project at hand was to replace the bottom of the cabinet under the kitchen sink. All the soaps, and cleansers, and sprays...all the little CoolWhip containers with scouring pads and sponges, miscellaneous unmatched bits and pieces of "stuff"...all were in a jumble where the hardboard had gotten soft in the middle and had just fallen through like an under-the-sink sinkhole.

Simple enough to replace, right? Not so fast, Round-eyes. Sure, putting in a new bottom would be a piece of cake. Put in a scrap 2x6 across the back of the cabinet for a support (I had saved some pieces from a building project for just such a purpose), then get a 1x12, cut it to the right depth and just lay it in. But then I remembered: a 1x12 is neither 1 inch thick nor 12 inches wide; so, although the first three pieces fit neatly together, I was left with a 2 1/4 " gap. Back to Home Depot for a 1x4, which I had to cut freehand to fit the remaining space. Whew!

Then, I had to deal with the reason *why* the bottom collapsed. There was obviously a substantial leak that had developed somewhere. (Look! There's a loose lock nut that seems to be the source. I'll just tighten that and...Drat! The plastic lock nut has split, and will have to be replaced. Another trip to Home Depot turns up two sizes of lock nuts to choose from...I'll get one of each and bring the other back later. Good thinking, huh?)

Meanwhile, back under the sink, I discover that the broken nut will have to be cut off...and that the new part will not fit over the flange that has to fit into the "J" shaped thingamabob that makes up the trap. Well...I'm a college graduate, so this time, while back at Home Depot, I get the whole set of parts, the connector, the trap, the out-pipe the lock nuts and washers; and, with my jaw set manfully and ready to do battle, I return home to resume the obeisant posture of one about to address the Lord of the Undersink. "I'm almost there," I think.

One of Murphy's Laws states "Standard and interchangeable parts...aren't." And I've proved that law yet again. Nothing fits...and the out-pipe requires an adapter...and...well, you get the idea. Not only that, but the day was gone and suppertime was upon us. Or, rather, Lyn was ready to eat out, since the kitchen sink was inoperable and cooking out of the question.

My friend Paul the Plumber came and fixed everything this morning in less than an hour.

I've found that a lot of life's ventures are like that. We have a project thrust upon us, take our best shot at dealing with it, only to have it "turn to prunes," as one of my friends used to say. The adversary's imps work their little pranks, trying to thwart our efforts and otherwise do their best to make us frustrated and miserable. They seem to know where our hot buttons are.

When that happens—and it happens a lot—I've learned to call on the spiritual Master Plumber to make all my failed Saturday Projects successful and rewarding. He has all the right equipment and knows just what to do...and He's always ready, just listening for my call.

Have you called on Him lately? He's waiting to hear from you— and He's in The Book.

Parable of The Great Escape

"Clippo the Clown" has been a member of the family for decades. He had already been an adopted sibling when my wife was a small child—perhaps even earlier, I'm not sure. My father-in-law was deeply interested in theater arts, especially marionettes, and I understand that he and my mother-in-law spent some of their courtship and early marriage going to puppet theater shows, workshops and seminars.

Clippo was once part of a whole troupe of marionettes, but the years have separated him from his high-strung companions. In fact, poor Clippo spent most of the last part of the twentieth century packed up in a box for safe keeping, seeing the light of day only on those rare occasions when he was taken out and studied as a curiosity by friends and neighbors; children, grandchildren and great-grandchildren.

Then, several years ago, while I was trying to think of something special we could give my mother-in-law as a gift, I had a great idea. Why not find a way to display Clippo so she could enjoy the memories of those days any time she wanted?

I found a suitable unfinished frame, built a shadow-box for it and set about devising a display that would do justice to the history of Clippo. I draped a swatch of red velvet across the back of the box to serve as a stage curtain. Then I attached Clippo to a block of wood painted to look like a trunk.

Clippo was arranged in a seated position on the block, with his hands placed in such a way that he appeared to be untying the strings attached to his feet. One of his legs was already untied and was hanging out of the frame. The strings for his hands, arms, legs, and torso hung from above, having already apparently been untied. He was almost free!

I intended to have a little brass plaque made, reading "The Great Escape," but I ran out of time, my deeds once more failing my intentions. The gift was a success anyway, though.

I'm not sure why the image of Clippo's Great Escape occurred to me this morning, but as I projected that picture on the video screen on the inside of my forehead, it gradually dawned on me that so much of one's life is spent just like Clippo...bound up by conventions and convictions and compulsions...constantly required to respond to the pulls and pressures of circumstances ...forced to answer and counter rather than to ask and to initiate action.

I truly believe that the measure of a successful life doesn't depend upon how well one responds to the pulls on the emotional, psychological, social and other strings that support and guide one in the learning stages of one's youth. Rather it is measured by the degree to which we mature and free ourselves of those strings, and begin to take into our own hands the meaningful living of life.

While in the security of those strings, we are intended to absorb the learning and wisdom and self-assurance they afford. Then comes the time to begin to free ourselves from the knots that bind us to the comfortable past and begin to strike out in reasoned paths of our own.

Look around at the people about you. Watch their actions. Listen to their arguments. It isn't difficult to discern those whose strings are worked by others, moving to the tunes sung and the words recited by others. They have become too well-adapted to the tyranny of those strings.

The Lord's plan for His people is that they should follow His Word, and find their freedom in its truth. We don't have to live like Clippo, either yielding to the yank of the strings or striving to loosen them by our own efforts. Jesus said, "If you hold to my teaching, you are really my disciples. Then you will know the truth, and the *truth* will set you free."

Did you get that? We needn't free ourselves. Truth unties the knots for us. Now, that is a Great Escape worth joining in on, along with countless millions who have already joined Him.

Are you ready to make a break for it?

Parable of The Autoharp

After fifteen years or so of teaching various ages in Sunday School, I decided to make a change. Well...to be more accurate, because our youngest daughter was having a tough time adjusting to Miss Connie's Three-Year-Old Sunday School class, I volunteered as a helper to make her feel more at home there.

As a result, I sat on the floor with Miss Connie's three-year-olds for ten years. At least, I sat with those who were willing to sit still for a few minutes at a time. We sang the songs—and I helped tell the Bible stories—that are the familiar tools of pre-school Sunday School teachers.

The singing time was one of the things they were especially fond of, because, for the first time in the young lives of most of them, they had the chance to make real music. The secret of my success in this was the use of an Autoharp.

For the uninitiated, the Autoharp is a zither-shaped instrument with 32 strings. Mounted above the strings is a device made up of a series of bars, each having felt pads arranged to damp out all strings except those needed to sound a specific chord. When each bar is pressed and the strings are strummed, only the strings of that selected chord will play, making a musical sound.

That explains why the Autoharp is so perfect for use with children. When they play with most musical instruments, the piano for instance, what do they get? Noise...or at best one or two random notes that don't sound very musical. When they blow on a horn, if they get any sound at all it's just a blat...or a squawk...or a screech... certainly not music. Only through careful teaching and faithful practice can they produce anything besides noise.

Not so with the Autoharp. Even three-year-olds can press a bar, strum the strings and produce real music...by themselves...with the first attempt. What a victory!

Another thing they learn very quickly is the distinction between discord and harmony ...between music and noise. I would strum the strings without pressing a chord bar and ask, "What is that sound?" They would chorus, "That's noise!" And then, with the perverse delight of three-year-olds, they would shout, "Do it again!"

It didn't take them long, however, to realize that pressing the chord bar before strumming was a lot more satisfying. "That's music," they would volunteer, and soon come to admit that making music was a lot more fun than merely making noise.

Nowadays there are multitudes of battery-operated gadgets that can produce musical sounds, but at that time the Autoharp was about all that was available. And making music on Mr. Jack's Autoharp was for many of them the beginning of an interest in music that has lasted for many years.

As I think about my life, and what I have observed about the lives of others, I am convinced that there is an application of the principle of the Autoharp. I realize that I have spent a lot of my time strumming the open strings, hoping that something harmonious would come out of my honest, sincere efforts...only to find that those efforts only produced "noise." And, if you will be honest with yourself, I think you'll have to admit that your life has its noisy times, too.

However, the more I study the Scriptures, and the more of life's testing times I endure, the more I realize that the Lord has provided my life "instrument" with all the chord bars I shall ever need to bring harmonious peace to every situation in which I find myself. And sometimes, when I can't seem to strike the correct chord, He even reaches down Himself and—much like Mr. Jack did for his three-year-olds—will press down the proper bar in order to keep up the flow of His perfect, soothing, spirit-healing music...as I continue in His service.

Parable of The Birthday Flight

For a number of years I have told my family I would really like to take a flight in an old-fashioned, open cockpit biplane. There's an airport near our home that advertises "Biplane Adventures," flights in one of these romantic aircraft. They have two of them that have been painstakingly restored and maintained, and they stay booked up much of the year.

These charter trips, up to an hour or so in duration, aren't really so expensive, especially considering the excitement and thrill of the experience, but I've always decided to wait until we could better afford it. That's why our children got together and pooled resources to give me a Biplane Ride Gift Certificate for my birthday last summer.

After planning for just the right time and season for my flight, I finally got it scheduled. It was still the tender, green part of Spring. The days were warming up nicely. In short, the timing was just about perfect.

The morning of my flight started out slightly overcast, but by the time they had rolled the beautiful, orange biplane onto the tarmac, the clouds were beginning to break up and the sun was starting to take charge of the day.

As I donned my cloth helmet, with its goggles and earphones, I felt every bit like one of those barnstorming adventurers I used to envy in the Saturday movie matinees I attended with such religious fervor as a boy.

With a touch of the switch, the pilot started the engine...first, a brief insistent whir and then, not the steroid-enhanced roar of a modern aircraft, but what I thought at the time sounded like a confident, manly growl that hardly varied in tone and pitch throughout the flight.

As we taxied away from the terminal, I flashed what I imagined was a boyish grin, waved and gave a "thumbs up" (you know, like Gary Cooper in the movie *Wings*) to the loved ones looking on in admiration as I set off on my brave adventure. At least, that's how I remember it.

It was all I had hoped it would be. Even better, because, to be honest, I didn't know for certain if I would become queasy, or feel like I was going to die at any minute. However, even the occasional air pocket that caused a sudden drop or boost, and the deep, rollercoaster-like turns were exhilarating and did nothing to spoil the overwhelming joy of floating purposefully above the familiar landscape.

I have told several folks since the flight that it had only one draw-back. At my age my skin has lost some of its elasticity. That's why it'll probably take several weeks for me to get that boyish grin off my face. I suppose that's a small price to pay, though.

That birthday flight was even more timely than I could have imagined, however. In the last week I have participated in two memorial services for wonderful Christians in the church where I serve. As I led the congregation in singing great songs of faith,

"Victory in Jesus" and "I'll Fly Away," I couldn't help but picture the two honorees.

I could visualize them both comfortably and securely strapped into that open cockpit, smiling to their families and friends, waving and giving them the thumbs up signal that all was well. We were all there, standing at the terminal, with mixed feelings of sadness...joy...thanksgiving, but still cheering them on, singing encouragement.

That is what it will be like, you know, for everyone who knows the Great Pilot. We'll go taxiing down the airstrip and suddenly we'll lift off, we'll float above the toil, discomforts, and pain of life and soar to that "land that is fairer than day." Now *that's* a flight I look forward to.

Parable of The Goldfish

I'm not sure where I came across this bit of trivia, but I recall hearing that goldfish have an incredibly short memory span. Just to be sure I remembered correctly I looked it up on Google. (There was a time when I would have had to explain "Googling.") Sure enough, there it was: Scientists have determined that the memory span of a typical goldfish is about 3 seconds.

I tried to imagine what kinds of tests one would have to put those experimental goldfish through to determine how long, and how much the little guys could remember. I even pictured one of those 1940's black and white movies, with a man in a fedora hat and a trenchcoat, waving his blackjack at a frightened goldfish, shining a bright light into his eyes, and saying, "We have ways to make you talk," and the fish saying over and over, "But I don't remember!"

No...really, they had a truly scientific procedure using food, and aggression, and even mating situations, to learn that these fish have even a shorter memory span than the typical husband. But, after all, maybe it's a blessing which makes life in a fish tank more bearable.

As usual with these observations, there was a recent event that brought this topic to mind.

As my wife and I were enjoying our date night at a local restaurant, we saw and talked with a much loved Christian friend who had recently lost his dear wife to complications from a disease which she had battled for ten years or so. Her sweet spirit and gentle nature have been an inspiration to all who have come into contact with her over the years. And he and their son have spirits and natures that were a perfect match for hers.

They told us they planned to travel to a favorite place in New England that the family had visited each summer for many years. It is a place they had even planned to retire to when the time came. Our friend said that there would be many melancholy memories there, but he and his son were taking the trip anyway.

That's when it occurred to me what a mixed blessing the human capacity for memory can be. Memory is what makes it possible for us to perform routine acts with ease. We learn to walk, talk, brush our teeth, tie shoes or neckties because of the gift of memory. Musicians, artists and craftsmen are only able to perform creative skills because of memory. These observations I write are the result of memories reclaimed from the mental filing cabinet that I keep just inside my forehead.

Unfortunately there are also fearful and painful memories.

Psychologists tell us that humans have the ability to bury unpleasant memories in the back lot of our subconscious. Someone once said that is the reason mothers are willing to have more than one baby.

Occasionally those buried memories fester and result in mental disorders that can only be dealt with when they are brought back into our consciousness. For the most part, however, human memory is among the greatest of the Lord's blessings. Where would we be without recollections of beautiful scenes, sounds, and aromas we have experienced? The touch of a loved one's hand? The pleasant presence of dear family and friends? How can we appreciate the present, except by viewing it through the lens of memory?

Just as surely as the absence of a dear one brings pangs of pain and awareness of loss during the most sensitive of times, the ability to recall the sense of joy and peace that was a part of that relationship provides the only balm that can truly heal the hurt that separation brings.

That is the great gift that the tiny goldfish can never experience. True, he won't have the sense of loss, or the fright that comes from the near disasters of life. But neither will he experience the blessings of reliving the joys of life, nor the soul-soothing spirit that alone can fill the void left by those who have departed from us. I suspect that those kinds of memories are intended by the Lord for humans only.

So don't envy the goldfish. Remember. Embrace once more what you thought was lost.

Parable of The Hand

The length of a hand. That's what made the difference between a gold and a silver medal in the Women's Olympic Swimming competition the other day. The American swimmer was a long-shot for a medal, anyway, I think, so the silver was welcome. But the gold was *almost* hers.

The hand is such an important measure for us as we go through life, isn't it? We have hand-print plaques on our walls, stacks of hand-prints traced in crayon, pen and pencil; all giving ample testimony to the presence and growth of children, grandchildren and "great-grands."

Scientists tell us that the hand, with its flexible fingers and opposable thumb is one of the defining physical characteristics of primates, especially good ol' *homo sapiens*. You know. Humans. People like you and me.

The human hand is remarkable in the infinite variety and range of operations it can perform. It can pluck a hair, a flower or a violin string. It can grip a hammer to drive a nail in the building of a house, or grip the drive lever of a bulldozer and push that house down.

Hands are capable of the most delicate tasks, from surgery on the brain to the scribing of the fine lines that become the etched strokes of an artistic masterpiece. They are useful for delivering tender caresses to the face of a loved one, as well as clenching in anger to deliver painful blows to any who threaten our peace and well-being. We even use our palms from time to time as places to write those important names and numbers we want to remember.

The fingers and thumb are effective means of communication as well. No one has to tell you the meaning of a "thumbs up" or a "thumbs down." One is good, the other is bad news. The index finger can be an indication of approval and selection, or it can be a sign of accusation.

The ring finger is the place where we often show signs of our personal commitments, either to another individual or to some group, such as a college, club or lodge. Sometimes those ring fingers are adorned to show that we have style or social status. Even the lowly pinky finger is occasionally lifted to make a show of gentle breeding and good manners.

References to the hands convey many kinds of impressions. "Mano a mano" means hand to hand and implies a manly conflict. Both hands held high indicate surrender...the right hand held up is a sign that we come in peace, empty-handed. One hand held high, closed into a fist challenges "Try and make me!"

The Bible, too, has many references to hands, especially the Hands of God. Among my favorites is verse seven in the Ninety-fifth Psalm, which says, "we are...the sheep of His hand." That was an expression that referred to pets that were especially loved and cared for.

Another Psalm that reminds me of God's gentle Hand is Psalm 3:3, where David says, "But Thou, O Lord, art...the lifter up of mine head." When I read that verse I remember times when as a boy I was hurt, or sad, or troubled, and my mother would tenderly place her mother-soft hand under my downcast chin and lift up my head to look into her loving blue eyes as she spoke those words of comfort and encouragement that brought the sunshine back into my day.

God's Word speaks vividly about His Hand smiting His foes, as well as lifting up, hiding and protecting His chosen ones. He leads us by His mighty Hand, and, perhaps most reassuring of all, Jesus promised that the adversary could never snatch even one of the elect from His Hand.

But who could deny that the most beautiful hands of all are the rugged, strong carpenter's hands of Jesus. The hands that were pierced in the process of atoning for our sin. That's why Isaiah 49:15b-16a strikes a stirring resonance in my heart: "But I will not forget you. See, I have engraved you on the palms of my hands." Our names on His Hand so He won't forget us. Wow!

Parable of The Life Kit

There we were...standing in an aisle of the toy department of the local Target store, with a Christmas shopping list in one hand and the cell phone in the other. We were doing our usual last-minute shopping for the grandchildren, were down to the last two or three and had run out of ideas. So we had called our youngest daughter for some emergency assistance.

She had gone over a number of things that Alex had asked for, but we had no luck finding any of them, until she said, "He does like those Lego sets, and he did want one of the Star Wars kits, but I don't remember which one it was." Hang up the phone. Begin stalking the aisles for Star Wars Lego doo-dahs of some sort. Find one, buy it, take it home, wrap it up, give it for Christmas... He loved it. Chalk one up for the Grandparents.

For someone who grew up with Lincoln Logs, Tinker Toys and Erector Sets, these toys are fascinating. The detail and coloring are remarkable, the assembly is challenging and the completed figures that are the result of all that effort really do stimulate the imagination.

I was thinking about Alex and this incident the other day, and how he and his brothers, and sisters, too, really like these toys that take so much assembly before they can be played with. It reminded me of one Sunday's lesson from the Pastor's Box.

That particular Sunday, children came streaming down all the aisles, some "power walking," some skipping, some running like kids do, with elbows and knees flinging in every direction, to join the pastor on the steps to the platform for the weekly Children's Sermon. As they climbed over one another, striving to get as close to his side as possible, he asked, "Who has the Pastor's Box today?" Each week one child is given the box, in which he or she is to place a favorite thing...the only rule is that it cannot be anything alive, or recently deceased.

On this occasion, as he opened the box I heard the murmurs of appreciation from the children—from my location in the choir loft I seldom can actually see the children or their objects of wonder and interest. The pastor, father of two "all boy" boys, said, "I know what this is. It's a Bionicle." (More approving sounds from the collection of cherubs.)

For those who hadn't been exposed to this new wonder—including those of us in the congregation and choir without small children in the house—he explained that a Bionicle is a sort of action figure that comes in what I would call "kit" form, all the parts and pieces in a plastic container with a picture of the completely assembled figure on the outside.

"As far as I'm concerned," he continued, "there's only one problem with these Bionicle figures: You have to put them together before you can play with them." ("That's right." "Yeah, I hate that.") Then he went on, "But don't you see? That's the beauty of it! It's just like life." He talked about how God gives us life in a kit...it's not assembled—we have to put it together and experience it...and try to build something good out of it.

I like that illustration. Each of us is born with a Life Kit, not unlike that box of Lego pieces sorted by size, shape and color...or the collection of parts of various sorts. But, unlike the Bionicles, or the Star Wars Galactic Cruiser (or whatever it was), there are no pictures to go by...no detailed instructions showing how parts A and B go together. Only the owner's manual.

So in order to end up with a life that's reasonably close to what the Master Toymaker had in mind, we have the responsibility to study the instruction manual and follow it faithfully until life is finished. The manual for the faithful, of course, is the Bible. Some trust popular "Life for Dummies" books, but the only faithful and reliable guide...the only one guaranteed to bring us to the conclusion of an abundant life, comes from the Manufacturer. And we have His Word on it.

Parable of The Recalled Goods

Have you noticed that in recent years there has been a tremendous increase in all types of goods being recalled by the manufacturers? Sometimes these are voluntary...the producer has discovered a defect of some sort and has notified the public that such-and-such a product should be returned to the retail outlet where it was purchased; at no cost to the customer, of course.

Other times the recall is compulsory, forced upon the manufacturer by some Federal, State or Local watchdog agency, requiring items to be replaced or the price to be refunded due to some reported health or safety hazard. Consumer protection advocates are becoming more and more vocal in their defense of the buying public...or the safety of the universe...or something.

There are news reports of automobiles that catch on fire while parked...brakes that fail... engines that stall without warning...unsafe safety devices.

Last Christmas there were dozens of reports of toy shelves emptied of imported toys made or decorated with unhealthy levels of lead. Others have been recalled because of the potential danger of small magnets or other small parts being swallowed by toddlers.

A staggering amount of ground beef was recalled recently due to possible contamination by listeria...another time it was e coli... yet another time it was a panic caused by the discovery of Mad Cow Disease among the herd that had been butchered to make the hamburger patties.

A processing plant in rural Georgia was nearly put out of business because tons of peanut butter were deemed unfit to eat because of poorly cleaned equipment. Spinach farmers faced bankruptcy because bacteria in rainwater run-off had been absorbed by their growing plants.

In one sense it's reassuring to realize that there are agencies whose sole purpose is to discover real or potential threats to the safety or health of the consuming public. However, in another sense it is sobering to see the number of ways that careless mistakes or thoughtless errors can pose serious problems, both physically and financially, for individuals, communities and even entire segments of the economy.

These recalls are so frightening, and make up such a large part of current events reporting, that it almost makes one pine for the days when we weren't so well informed about such things. You know…"ignorance is bliss."

The interesting thing is that without these reports we would look at the advertising, the attractive packaging, the creative displays, and take them at their face value. We would assume that everything was alright because the container or box was clean, the store environment was spotless and appeared sanitary. And the pictures of the contents *are* so appealing, aren't they?

This is another evidence of how much we value the outward appearance—the nicely designed wrapper, if you please—in judging the appeal, character and quality of the individuals with which we come in contact. As the Bible warns, "Man looketh on the outward appearance, but the Lord looketh on the heart." (I Samuel 16:7)

Our God knows how easily we are influenced by the marketing techniques of the world—how strongly drawn we are by powerful advertising messages and public relations strategies. This is a fact whether they are used in commerce or in personal relationships.

We can be easily fooled by appealing wrappers of religiosity and benevolence, by persuasive arguments about what seems right and good; when the reality is that they are chosen to disguise ideas and motives that can prove harmful to those who take them too seriously.

I am comforted by the knowledge that I can rely upon the Creator to be faithful in issuing a recall warning when the contents are not what they should be; or to certify them as trustworthy and reliable. It is our duty and privilege to strive to be approved. With Christ in our hearts that approval is guaranteed. Without Him, recall is inevitable...and lasts for eternity.

Parable of Seed Versus Sod

I try to take a walk around the lake in our subdivision two or three times a week. The best time for me is first thing in the morning, about 7:30 or so. A while back, as I was walking around the far side of the lake, I passed a house that I have admired since we first moved into the neighborhood, and noticed that a lot of landscaping was under way.

The old lawn had been completely been roto-tilled, and the process of laying down a new sod lawn was well under way. Over to one side I counted twelve pallets of sod, each patiently awaiting its turn—as only sod can—to be carefully placed by the hard-working band of workers.

I recognized the name on the landscaper's truck to be that of a friend of ours from church, and the next time I saw him I told him what a good job they had done with those twelve pallets of sod. "That wasn't even half of it," he said with a chuckle. "In all, we put down a total of 27 pallets. When they said they wanted a lawn, they meant they wanted a lawn *today*."

Not too long after that, a large new house—maybe it would better be classed as an estate—was built around the corner from that same subdivision. The first that we were aware anything was going up was when every tree, bush, shrub and plant was cut, chopped, dug and scraped away over a two-day period.

Within a surprisingly short time a lovely house was completed, resting the middle of the flattest, neatest swept-dirt yard you ever saw. We all thought, "Oh, if only they had left some trees! It looks so barren and forlorn with nothing but red Georgia dirt on all sides."

Then the miraculous transformation occurred. I came by one afternoon to see several truckloads of trees balled in burlap, pallets of sod and countless plants of all types and sizes in pots and flats piled and stacked around the edge of the lot. In less than a week, the trees were planted and mulched, shrubs and flowers were planted in a well designed landscape plan that was pleasing to see. It was lovely. Instant landscape. No pain, no delay...if one has the money.

Excuse me, please, but these two examples illustrate what I see as a symptom of a serious personality flaw afflicting our society today. And I'm not the only one to recognize the dangerous threat it poses for our future. I've heard others make the same lament.

Instant gratification. "Don't postpone the enjoyment." "Fly now, pay later." "Charge it today and pay for it with next month's dollars...they'll be cheaper then." "You mean you don't use Instant Messaging? How retro!" "Next week!? Can't I have it today?"

We even tend to approach our Christian witnessing with this same attitude. We act as if we expect the Holy Spirit to come along with His spiritual roto-tiller, dig up the deep-rooted sin, scrape it all away, lay down some spiritual sod and "bing-bang-boom you're a Christian."

For countless millennia people had no choice but to prepare the soil, plant the seed, watch over the tender seedlings, pull weeds, fight insects and wait for the lawn to fill in the bare spots and grow high enough for us to mow. It took work, it took discipline and it took faith that our efforts would one day show the desired result. And sometimes it took years!

I'm not sure that people thought of laying sod 2,000 years ago, but, even if they had such a practice, I'm certain that Jesus' parable of the sower wouldn't have changed, because He of all people understood the importance of the personal effort and commitment necessary to affect the desired spiritual change that leads to the productive life of a Christian disciple.

Laying sod is great for lawns. But it's terrible for producing active, effective Christians. It takes time, hard work and serious commitment to the development of personal relationships to accomplish that. However, the results last a lifetime...and they're guaranteed for eternity.

Parable of The Electric Pickles

It started out as a joke, really. I was trying to encourage the newly formed Youth Praise Team to come up with a distinctive name. I said, "It should be a reasonably serious, meaningful name. One that will be clever, but also enduring. Not anything too cute or too frivolous."

I went on to give a couple of "bad" examples from my past experiences with teenagers. I told them about the time the youth from our church in Atlanta came back from Church Camp. They had been divided into two teams and each team was to come up with its own name.

One team called itself the Super Jews, which appealed to my adman's mind, once they explained that, since they were followers of Jesus—born a Jew, and yet Son of God—they were, in fact, part of the family of new and improved, or "Super" Jews. Perhaps a bit frivolous to adult minds, but consistent with the teens' spiritual sense.

The other team came up with a name that didn't seem to have any other rationale than to be outrageous and silly. They suggested the name "The Electric Pickles."

"What is *that* supposed to mean?" the adults all asked, recoiling slightly, like a snail's antenna when it touches something unexpected. "Can't you think of something with a little more *spiritual* depth to it?" But the teeners stuck to their choice, and thus "The Electric Pickles" they became—at least until Camp was over.

Now, I knew better than to have brought up those two examples of the "wrong" kind of name. I really did. But I did it anyway. I said,"... and you surely don't want to choose something crazy like 'The Super Jews' or 'The Electric Pickles.'"

Silly me. Would you be even a little surprised to learn that their first choice for a name was "The Electric Pickles"? Not if you have ever spent any time with teenagers.

The truth is that they were just having a little fun with their stodgy old leader, but their enthusiasm for that name started me thinking.

Exactly what *is* a pickle, anyway? I looked it up, and began to get a little excited about the idea myself. Let me take a few phrases out of the dictionary under the heading of "pick-le (*n*) 1. Any edible product...that has been preserved and flavored. A solution...for preserving and flavoring. 2. ...(a) solution used as a bath to remove (surface impurities) ...(prior to) finishing." Check it out. I don't think you'll find that I did any injustice to the definition by lifting these portions out of context.

Here, then, is the picture that came to my mind: A Christian is the physical manifestation of a soul that has been preserved to eternal life by being submerged in the Grace of God. It not only preserves, but adds flavor to life...and distinguishes that life from those not so preserved.

And just as a pickling solution works to remove impurities from the surface of metals to which it is applied, the Christian life exerts an influence upon those with whom it comes into contact. It works to bring about cleansing and is used, by the power of the Holy Spirit, to prepare those lives for the finishing process of salvation.

On top of that, the idea of electrifying anything suggests the possibility of a source of power and energy not previously available, but now accessible to all who will simply plug into it. We talk of a powerful speaker "electrifying" a crowd...exciting them...stirring them up.

And when electricity is added to the pickling process, that makes it much more efficient and effective. In fact, electrical power is what makes possible the mass production of the finely finished articles that stock showroom floors and store shelves.

Doesn't "electric pickling" suggest what witnessing should be like? Christians sharing Christ in the power and energy of the Holy Spirit, slowing spiritual decay, giving an exciting flavor and adding a perfect finish to a life?

Maybe "The Electric Pickles" isn't such a bad name after all. What do you think?

INDEX

Parable of	Page No.
A Bumper Sticker Philosophy	84
A Certain Sound	166
A Certain Sound - Our Journey Together	169
A Fellow Named Fred	122
A House Deserted	106
A House Deserted - Moved On	109
A Name That Is Known	170
A Summer's Lightning	81
First Things	163
One Who Would Lead	20
One Who Would Lead - Part 2	22
Pals and Puppies	26
Patchwork	32
Persistence	69
Proper Etiquette	72
Seed Versus Sod	276
The Appointed Time	247
The Autoharp	258
The Believable Mr. Ripley	214
The Best Intentions	154
The Big Idea	157
The Birthday Flight	261
The Brick	11
The Cats	75

The Cats - Part 2	78
The Cheerful Giver	160
The Cow Paths	103
The Cows and the Kids	14
The Devil Dog	87
The Distant Spot	235
The Drownproofer	42
The Dumpster Diver	151
The Ego Pruners	17
The Electric Pickles	279
The Falling Rain	241
The Goldfish	264
The Good and Old	125
The Good and Old, In Memory of	128
The Great Escape	255
The Hand	267
The Hazardous Ones	130
The Heartbeat	133
The Insistent Input	196
The Jar of Fleas	45
The Jesus Lizard	211
The Last Chance	225
The Lasting Love	48
The Leaders of Cheer	51
The Life Coach	205
The Life Kit	270
The Little Cat Who Could	110
The Meaningful Life	113
The Mountain Man	116
The Near Miss	226
The Not Dead	229
The One In Charge	232
The Open Hand	173
The Pastor's Box	29
The Pocket Full	136
The Poem	35
The Poem - The Way to Win	38

The Power of the Petty	176
The Questioned Answer	179
The Quiet Call	238
The Recalled Goods	273
The Risk Taker	182
The Sanctified Ones	185
The Saturday Project	252
The Secure Son	139
The Shared Blessing	39
The Shared Light	188
The Signal Light	90
The Smooth Stone	54
The Soup Pot	199
The Special Touch	202
The Steeple	244
The Table Lamp, the Teacup and the Ladder-back Chair	58
The Talents	61
The Tears	119
The Things We Do	142
The Tigers and the Gnats	64
The Turtle Shell	208
The Unclouded Day	148
The Undetected Input	190
The Un-Question	220
The Waiting Ones	145
The Well-Chosen Word	94
The Wrong Goal	217
Things Remembered	97
Traveling with Mom	100
Trombones and Tomatoes	193
Underwater Safety	60

CPSIA information can be obtained at www.ICGtesting.com
Printed in the USA
239096LV00002B/2/P